THE REVOLUTION
OF TENDERNESS

Being a Catholic

in today's Church

RAYMOND FRIEL

redemptorist
p u b l i c a t i o n s

Published by **Redemptorist Publications**
Alphonsus House, Chawton, Hampshire, GU34 3HQ, UK
Tel. +44 (0)1420 88222, Fax. +44 (0)1420 88805
Email rp@rpbooks.co.uk, www.rpbooks.co.uk

A registered charity limited by guarantee
Registered in England 3261721

Copyright © Redemptorist Publications 2016
First published January 2016

Text by Raymond Friel
Edited by Finola Robinson
Designed by Eliana Thompson
Photos/Illustrations: Shutterstock, p233 Lucas Cranach the Younger [Public domain], via Wikimedia Commons

ISBN 978-0-85231-436-4

A CIP catalogue record for this book is available from the British Library.

The publisher gratefully acknowledges permission to use the following copyright material:

Excerpts from the New Revised Standard Version of the Bible: Anglicised Edition, © 1989, 1995, Division of Christian Education of the National Council of the Churches of Christ in the United States of America. Used by permission. All rights reserved.

Printed by Portland Print,
Kettering NN16 6UN

Acknowledgements

I would like to thank Sandra Gormley for transcribing the interviews with such efficiency and understanding; the governors of Saint Gregory's Catholic College for their support; my editors Finola Robinson and Caroline Hodgson for their patience and precision and all the team at Redemptorist Publications for their professionalism, humour and creativity; the twelve for their time and generosity of spirit in the interviews; and as always my wife Janet, for love and forbearance.

By the same author

Seeing the River (Edinburgh: Polygon, 1995)

Renfrewshire in Old Photographs, with Richard Price (Glasgow: Mariscat, 2000)

Stations of the Heart (Cambridge: Salt, 2008)

Southfields Vols 1-6, ed. with Richard Price (London: Southfields Press)

PS Nos 1-7, ed. with Richard Price (London: Richard Price)

How to Survive Working in a Catholic School, with Sister Judith Russi (Chawton: Redemptorist Publications, 2013)

How to Survive in Leadership in a Catholic School (Chawton: Redemptorist Publications, 2015)

Dedication

For Ellen Friel – loving mother, beloved disciple.

You must give up your old way of life; you must put aside your old self, which gets corrupted by following illusory desires. Your mind must be renewed by a spiritual revolution so that you can put on the new self that has been created in God's way, in the goodness and holiness of the truth.

Ephesians 4:22-24

CONTENTS

FOREWORD

There is a passage in Evelyn Waugh's *Brideshead Revisited* where the beautiful but exasperating Lady Julia Flyte explains to her lover Charles Ryder, the narrator of the novel, why she cannot be his wife. She was married in the Catholic Church to the no-good philanderer Rex Mottram, and though the marriage broke down for obvious reasons, as far as she and the Church were concerned that was it. This is in fact Waugh's cameo portrait of mid-twentieth-century Roman Catholicism – the novel was published in 1945 – and Waugh, I think, expects us to admire her, and it. And in a way I do.

She explains her reasoning to an uncomprehending Ryder:

> "I've always been bad. Probably I shall be bad again, punished again. But the worse I am, the more I need God. I can't shut myself out from his mercy... I saw today there was one unforgivable thing... the bad thing I was on the point of doing, that I'm not quite bad enough to do; to set up a rival good to God's."

She goes on: "If I give up this one thing I want so much," then, "However bad I am, He won't quite despair of me in the end."

It is right to respect her spirit of sacrifice, of putting obedience to the laws of the Church before her own interests. But the passage also describes a lost world of Catholic spirituality, where the absolute priority is about avoiding the wrath of an angry God. Julia is deeply, deeply convinced of her own sinfulness. And mortal sin

– which destroys one's relationship with God completely – is always only a tiny step away. She is truly guilt-ridden; in her maudlin despair she thinks she is worthless. There is every chance, incidentally, that her marriage to Mottram could have been annulled and she could have married her true love Charles Ryder anyway – but she needs and deserves to be punished, so easy ways out are not for her. And it has to be said, her stalwart faith impresses Ryder, and contributes to his own eventual decision to convert. The lesson surely is that even desperate situations are never without the possibility of grace, when God is always free to act. He will make good use of the most unpromising material.

And that is true of another twentieth-century Catholic novel, *Brighton Rock* by Graham Greene, which also takes us deep into the unconscious dreads of a generation which now seems so remote from us. It is symptomatic of a certain style of Catholicism that with various murders and other crimes on his conscience, Pinkie is most worried by his false marriage to the girl Rose, yet another mortal sin for which to be damned. It was against the law of the Church, and the power of the Church is not to be mocked.

"Do you go to Mass?" he asked.

"Sometimes," Rose said. "It depends on work. Most weeks I wouldn't get much sleep if I went to Mass."

"I don't care what you do," the Boy said sharply. "I don't go to Mass."

"But you do believe, don't you?" Rose implored him, "You think it's true?"

"Of course it's true," the Boy said. "What else could there be?" he went scornfully on. "Why," he said, "It's the only thing that fits. These atheists, they don't know nothing. Of course there's Hell, Flames and damnation," he said with his eyes on the dark shifting water and the lightning and the lamps going out above the black struts of the Palace Pier, "Torments."

"And Heaven too," Rose said with anxiety, while the rain fell interminably on.

"Oh, maybe," the Boy said, "Maybe."

This Catholic Church of Waugh's and Greene's time is not a tender place, and the mercy of God is thin gruel compared with the eternal punishment he has in mind for those who break the rules. The worst thing to be, in this world, is a "bad Catholic", which Pinkie clearly is and Julia is terrified of becoming. But Pinkie still wants somehow to be saved. Even as the noose tightens round his neck – "between the stirrup and the ground" – he hopes to be able to cry out like the Good Thief on the cross. Is that hope the fruit of God's grace and is it enough? Greene leaves us wondering.

(I do sometimes wonder whether we are losing the dark side of Catholicism, the cadences of the *Dies Irae* – the sense that "It is a fearful thing to fall into the hands of the living God." Maybe we can get it back, without having to return to the dark days of *Brighton Rock*.)

The fundamental dichotomy between good and bad Catholics was particularly strong in English Catholicism right up until the Second Vatican Council. Its origins lay in the sixteenth-century Council of Trent, which launched the Counter-Reformation and moulded Catholic culture in the centuries afterwards. It was no doubt a defence mechanism against the constant pressure to compromise during what were called the Penal Times, where the English State and Church used every means to break the will of the dwindling and beleaguered Catholic population, to try to get it to abandon its obstinate ways and conform. The circumstances which gave rise to it have passed, but it still casts its shadow. The message is that even on the way to heaven, you are on the brink of hell. One false step and you are doomed. Only strict observance of all the rules can protect you.

Brideshead was published only twenty years before Vatican II, and the Catholic world beginning to emerge after 1965 was sharply different from what had gone before. In the novel *How Far Can You Go?* David Lodge gently teases the freedom young Catholics were suddenly feeling, in his account of a conversation between them in a group which called itself Catholics for an Open Church.

> "Where we went wrong, of course," said Adrian, "was in accepting the theology of mortal sin."
>
> "No," said Miriam, who had been listening quietly to their comments. "Where you went wrong was in supposing that the Church belonged to the Pope or the priests instead of to the People of God."
>
> They nodded agreement. "The People of God" was a phrase the Catholics for an Open Church approved of. It made them sound invincible.

These three novels would make useful background reading to Raymond Friel's study of modern Catholicism. He is clearly not writing about a finished article but a work in progress, a transitional phase in the life of the Catholic Church.

Unless we understand what went before, we will not understand what is emerging in its place. This is particularly true of the post-council period from the mid 1970s onwards, under the papacies of St John Paul II and Benedict XVI. In a sense the first Polish pope never left Poland, for he continued to see both the world and the Church through a Polish lens. Neither the Reformation nor the Enlightenment had such deep effects in Poland as they did in western Europe; and the early life of Karol Wojtyla was spent under a succession of cruel and brutal tyrannies – first occupation by the Nazis and then the takeover by the Communists. He had never lived under a democracy.

John Paul's instinctive reaction to the troubles afflicting the Church when he became pope was to reapply the spiritual discipline of the Counter-Reformation, just as a pre-war prince bishop in Poland would have done, in order to impose a return to the values of the Catholicism of Julia and Pinkie. He was the best of popes and the worst of popes. It is clear that the present pope, Francis, is engaged in trying to reverse the effects of the worst, and building on the strengths of the best. Pope John Paul II was a brilliant moderniser of Catholic social teaching, even as he took Catholic moral theology backwards. Above all, Pope Francis wants a church which shows forth the mercy of God, not by enforcing a set of rules but by the touch of a kindly tender Person who encounters us at the level of our deepest needs.

I say a work in progress and not a finished job, because there is a monumental task still ahead and hardly yet started, to discover a way of being Catholic that no longer relies on rules but on love. Raymond Friel is fully engaged in that task in this book, and I would only want to add two contributions of my own to the thoughts and suggestions he is offering.

The first concerns prayer. The advice he offers on meditation and contemplation is highly relevant to the search for a modern lay spirituality. I would just add something I first heard from Cardinal Basil Hume, something he learnt no doubt in the cloisters of his Benedictine abbey and in his favourite other place, the rugby field. Compare, he said, what it feels like to be silent and alone in a room, with what it feels like to be in the presence of someone else, someone you deeply care for, in that same room – but still silent. The similarity may be in the absence of speech, but the two experiences are otherwise utterly different. Just try it and see.

To be in that person's presence in the profoundest way, you don't have to be talking to them all the time. You may say nothing. Being together with them, in their company, is what does it. You are, so to speak, in communion with them, sharing a spiritual and emotional space. And this, said Hume, is like putting oneself in the presence of God. He is always in that room with you, whether you speak together or not. Indeed, it seems foolish to fret that one is not using words; they are not necessary.

My second suggestion is also not far from Raymond Friel's. Many Catholics are bothered and perplexed when told they need to have a personal relationship with Jesus Christ. It sounds almost as if they are being asked to make Jesus a kind of imaginary friend. That sounds too much like indulging in a fantasy. But there is another approach. Put very simply: using the Gospels. Obtain a good translation – there is sound advice in this book – and then settle down and read it, page by page, chapter by chapter, book by book. You probably need to read most of it twice or more, and you will find you will want to.

But remember, these are four accounts of the life of Jesus, sometimes complementary, sometimes overlapping, sometimes contradictory, all of which were written a substantial period after his death. Don't take any of it too literally, therefore; allow for lapses of memory or misunderstandings by the authors, even occasional flights of fancy or intrusions into the text by unknown editors. It is not a book of rules. It does not define a creed or propose a philosophy. It is more like a storybook. Jesus, when he speaks, as he does mainly in parables, is not really talking to Catholics at all, but to fellow Jews. And bear in mind who the authors were, and what they were each trying to achieve.

Inevitably, if you follow this course, you will become more and more intrigued by the central character, even as if he were someone you had once met personally. He will become ever more familiar, like someone you have always known. I guarantee you will quickly think you do know him, and begin to see how his mind works. And you will, I am sure, want to learn from others how they have known him, to expand your appreciation. In a sense those four Gospels give us everything we need to know, provided we do not mistake them for a textbook.

What effect he has on you is up to you. I can't imagine it for you. Had Pinkie or Lady Julia followed this simple advice they wouldn't be who they were; their Catholicism would have meant something much larger and more life-giving than a book of rules for them to keep and a list of penalties if they dared break them. But even within that Catholicism, that all-embracing but stifling Catholic culture, God kept breaking through. He still does – as every page of this fascinating book bears witness.

We now have the privilege of being led away from that culture towards something better, richer, more loving and more tender. And more human.

Clifford Longley

Introduction

This book is for anybody who is interested in what it means to be a disciple of Jesus in the Catholic Church today. It is not an A–Z of Catholicism; there are plenty of those to choose from. My interest is in what I consider an important moment in the life of the Catholic Church – the transition from a "folk" Church of mass membership to a Church of intentional disciples; people who have made an adult choice to take Jesus seriously and try to live out the Gospel. My focus is not the great body of teaching of the Catholic Church, but rather what Pope Francis is trying to get us back to, namely the *kerygma* (literally "proclamation"), the core or the essence of our faith, which is the revelation of Jesus Christ as the mercy of the Father, the revelation of tenderness.

I do not have all the answers but I can share something of my experience and, better still, I can share the experience of twelve Catholics I had the privilege of interviewing in England and the Philippines. The twelve were not chosen after any kind of lengthy process of selection to ensure a faultlessly balanced view. They were people I knew or knew about who were willing to share their faith journey and reflections on the Church today. I offered them anonymity so that they could speak freely – some chose other names and some were happy to go by their own names. I started off wanting an equal split between male and female but was happy in the end to have seven women and five men, given the imbalance the other way for much of the Church's history.

I also wanted to hear from mostly lay people, since our voices have not been sufficiently heard in the Church and, in the West at least, where there are so few ordained clergy, we will have to assume more responsibility for the running of the Church in the years to come. Five of the twelve – Sr Mary John, Rebecca, Archie, Lirio and Jun – are based in the Philippines and the others in England. I felt it was important to get a broad view, as England is in many ways not representative of the Church today. The Church has always been a universal organisation but it has for much of its history been Eurocentric. Now it is entering a truly global phase and Catholics in the West must develop some understanding of the context and aspirations of their brothers and sisters in the developing world, where most Catholics now live.

I have offered suggestions for individual or group reflections at the end of each chapter if they are helpful. It is best if you read the chapters in order since there is some kind of a rationale in the sequence. I have suggested using a journal for individual reflections largely because that is my practice. Since I was in primary school I have kept a vade mecum – a notebook for jotting down interesting words and quotations, and the occasional insight of my own. The fruits of that habit you will find in the "Gems from the Treasure Box" throughout the book. Perhaps one or two suggestions in the "Resources for Further Study" at the end of each chapter might catch your eye and lead to some further study or growth in faith.

I have resisted the urge to produce a ten-point plan or the five steps to becoming an intentional disciple. That does not seem to me to ring true to the journey of faith. We have enough bullet points and action plans in our lives. Discipleship is not a checklist. There are certainly stages, but above all discipleship is an encounter and then a commitment, which is why I have concentrated so much on scripture; the place where we encounter the historical Jesus. He was not much into action plans either. He did not leave written memos for the disciples about what to do in every situation. He taught using stories and sayings, he taught in conversation, he taught in wonderful deeds.

So what gives me any right to go into print and talk about Jesus and the Catholic Church? For most of the history of the Church the public talking and published writing has been done by male clergy. It is a rich tradition but it is changing. We are now beginning to hear the voices of ordinary Catholics and that movement is critical for the future of the Church, I believe. I am not a theologian (although I am guided by them throughout this book) but I am a baptised disciple of Jesus in the Catholic Church and would like to share some of the pain and pleasure of that commitment. If the Church in the West is to have any future at all it will require lay men and women to grow in confidence and wisdom, to speak out, to share their experiences and to take on ministries of responsibility.

There have been times of darkness and confusion in my journey of faith. I have felt let down by the Church at times and at other times have reciprocated by letting the Church down. But I have hung in there and am glad I did because I believe that with Pope Francis and his successors the Church is on the verge of a new era of renewed commitment to living the Gospel message – radical, inspiring, counter-cultural – of our Lord and Saviour, Jesus Christ.

My father's books: from a "totally Catholic culture" to Vatican II and beyond

The Catholic Church was thrown from its horse on 25 January 1959, the Feast of the Conversion of Saint Paul. On that day Angelo Roncalli, better known to history as Pope John XXIII (now Saint John XXIII), announced to a small group of cardinals his intention to gather together all the bishops of the Church for the Second Vatican Council. In his opening address to the council some three years later, he recalled the moment when he broke the news to them: "The response was immediate. It was as though some ray of supernatural light had entered the minds of all present: it was reflected in their faces; it shone from their eyes." [1]

The reality was probably more human. It is not uncommon to hear the view that, later, many of those present voiced "concerns and objections".[2] Why were the cardinals concerned? Perhaps because very few people in the Church saw any need for a meeting of this kind. The Church of the mid twentieth century seemed strong, stable and eternal. Besides, the First Vatican Council (1869-1870) had defined the dogma of papal infallibility, so what was there to discuss?

When the amiable, portly Angelo Roncalli was elected pope in October 1958, following the long and conservative reign of Pope Pius XII, he was widely seen as an interim pope, a transitional figure who would bring a safe pair of hands to the job until the cardinals could find a candidate and direction they could agree on next time. Roncalli was in his late seventies and was not expected to occupy the Holy See for very long, nor do anything very interesting. The Holy Spirit had other ideas. What was so astonishing about John XXIII's announcement was that he was not responding to a groundswell of popular sentiment for reform. There was no great heresy that had to be denounced (*anathema*) as in previous councils. In the opening address, he put on record what prompted him to summon the bishops. It was not the conclusion of a long period of discernment or discussion, but rather the decision came to him "in a sudden flash of inspiration".[3] In another phrase often attributed to him, he wanted to throw open the windows of the Church and let the breeze of the Spirit disturb the dusty interior.

On 11 October 1962, after three years of busy preparation, around two thousand five hundred bishops processed solemnly into Saint Peter's Basilica in Rome under the sceptical eye of the world's media. John XXIII's opening address set the tone and is a remarkable document in itself. He dismissed the prophets of doom in the Church who, he said, could see "nothing but calamity and disaster in the present state of the world." The view that the modern world is going to hell in a handbasket can bring a kind of self-righteous comfort to those who believe they are going in the opposite direction, but that is not the view the Council adopted. John XXIII was optimistic, despite evidence to the contrary throughout history, speaking with confidence of "the hand of God ever directing men's efforts". The Church in the past had a focus on the salvation of souls, the individual soul (*cura animarum* – the care of souls) but now it was reaching out to the world and was just as concerned with the "material good of humanity".

The opening address of the Council was no less than a revolution in tone and attitude. The Church was often seen as a stern guardian of morality with a dogmatic resolution for every complex situation in the lives of people, but this pope sounded a new note. He preferred the "balm of mercy to the arm of severity" and called for a "new enthusiasm, a new joy". He wanted a new language to present old truths to the modern world: "For the deposit of faith… is one thing; the manner in which these truths are set forth (with their meaning preserved intact) is something else." This is an ongoing challenge for anyone involved in the Church: if we rely on the old language we will soon discover that no one is listening because they just don't understand what we are saying.

There was also groundbreaking outreach to other Christian denominations, as well as Jewish people and followers of the Muslim faith. Gone was the old language of blame, confrontation and separation, which many of us grew up with. In one of the shortest but most remarkable documents of the Council, *Nostra Aetate* (Declaration on the Relation of the Church to Non-Christian Religions), the Church finally deplored anti-Semitism in unambiguous language. According to John XXIII's address to the Council, here was the vision of a Church wanting to "show herself as a loving mother of all mankind: gentle, patient, and full of tenderness and sympathy for her separated children". John XXIII went further still and spoke to the whole human race, evoking the story from the Acts of the Apostles when Peter and John on their way to the Temple encounter the lame man begging for alms:

> Peter looked intently at him, as did John, and said: "Look at us." And he fixed his attention on them, expecting to receive something from them. But Peter said: "I have no silver or gold, but what I have I give you; in the name of Jesus Christ of Nazareth stand up and walk." And he took him by the right hand and raised him up; and immediately his feet and ankles were strong.

It was a bold choice of passage to illustrate the kind of church that the Pope wanted to emerge from the Council – a church which turns to the pleading world with an intense and loving gaze, sets the downtrodden back on their feet with a hand of friendship, and helps them to "understand their true nature and dignity and purpose". The message was clear: the primary gift the Church has to offer is the divine life, which alone bestows dignity on the individual.

In the course of four sessions between 1962 and 1965 sixteen documents were produced which together represent a "trajectory toward engagement with the world, openness to other Christians, affirmation of baptismal equality and appreciation for other religions".[4] It should be stressed that not everyone in the Catholic Church shares this positive view of the Council. For some so-called traditionalists, Vatican II was a colossal error, weakening the Church's message and mystique (see Paul's comments at the end of this chapter). But I think it's fair to say that the majority view is that Vatican II was a necessary *aggiornamento* ("bringing up to date") that has set the direction for the Church in the twenty-first century and is a body of work which anybody with any interest in the Church should, at some point, reflect on deeply. It was the Council which made the Church more attractive (or less "severe", as John XXIII said) without diluting any teaching, and for those on the threshold who may have negative memories of the Church, either from childhood or more recently, that might just be a way in, or a way back.

The Long Nineteenth Century

The period before Vatican II, from the papal reigns of Pius IX (1846–1878) to Pius XII (1939–1958), is sometimes known as the "long nineteenth century" of the Church; a monolithic period characterised by an emphasis on the eternal and unchangeable, a position which became more compelling as the pace of change in the secular world increased. In many ways the identity of the Church in those years was a reaction to the traumatic upheavals of the Reformation in the sixteenth century. The reformers, many of whose points are now seen as entirely reasonable, focused their attacks on the Pope, the priesthood and the sacraments. At the Council of Trent (1545–1563), the Church responded by defending and promoting those very things.

This led to a sustained concentration on the visible and structural aspects of the Church: the clergy, hierarchy and institution. It also led to an antipathy to all things "modern" and clear instructions to the faithful about what they could and could not believe or have anything to do with. In 1864 Pope Pius IX, who would later convene the First Vatican Council, published *The Syllabus of Errors*, a compendium of the most egregious moral errors of the day. The final "error" is the idea that: "The Roman Pontiff can, and ought to, reconcile himself, and come to terms with progress, liberalism and modern civilization."[5] The window was very firmly shut on the clamour of the modern world.

This focus on clergy, authority and hierarchy led to a very particular attitude towards the laity: the vast majority of the Church's membership who were not clergy or in religious orders. In his classic book, *The God of Surprises*, the Jesuit Gerard W. Hughes sums it up as follows:

17

> The way in which religion was often taught to Catholics... since the Council of Trent in the sixteenth century, namely through a catechism of questions and answers which were a summary of the very technical theological language contained in Trent's Council documents, encouraged Catholics to believe that religion is a subject which you were not expected to understand, but to which you must give your whole-hearted assent! This approach instilled a childish attitude with little or no encouragement to move beyond it.[6]

There was little room for debate or disagreement (see Tom's comments at the end of this chapter). The Church possessed the truth, the world was wicked, the purpose of our life on earth was to gain the rewards of life in heaven, where God lived in eternal glory, and at the same time avoid the nightmare of eternity in hell. The sacraments were the means to gain the grace required to avoid that fate. Every angle was covered, there was no such thing as privacy. As a young boy attending Mass with my parents in a cold church in Scotland, my first memories were of fierce crew-cut priests who knew how to paint hell in the most lurid colours. This was our main incentive for being good. If you ever get the chance to visit Rome, spend a morning at the Vatican Museum and you will see it for yourself. At the end of the tour when the crowds funnel into the Sistine Chapel, stand in front of Michelangelo's *Last Judgement* for as long as the guards will let you. As the currents of humanity flow around you, the drama of salvation and condemnation is enacted in vividly corporeal detail on the monumental frieze. The damned suffer horribly, for ever.

This hellish vision was not inspired by scripture, nor anything Jesus revealed to us about the nature of God, but by the fourteenth-century Italian poet Dante. In his *Inferno* there is a niche and a particular punishment for every manner of sinner. In the very depths, the ninth "circle" of hell, we find the traitors to their Lords: Brutus, Cassius and the one who walked the dusty tracks of Palestine with Jesus, the hapless

Judas Iscariot. Satan himself, the archetypal traitor, "tortured them for sin" and the poet seems to revel in the detail. Judas is being eaten alive perpetually from the front but that "is nothing to the claws that flayed his hide and sometimes stripped his back to the last flake".[7] This is one disciple who was never in any danger of forgiveness.

We suffered under the illusion of a sadistic God (or rather our projections of such a God) for the best part of eight hundred years and the imagination of clergy and laity alike was accordingly disfigured. In the twentieth century, James Joyce provided one of the last and most memorable examples of the "hellfire" sermon. The long, legendary rant of Father Arnall in *A Portrait of the Artist as a Young Man* is one of the reasons why the young intellectual Stephen Dedalus leaves behind the restrictions of Catholic Ireland to find freedom. You can't really blame him.

In theological terms there was a sharp separation, or dichotomy, between nature (which was fallen, corrupt) and grace (the life of God), which held sway for many centuries. As Margaret Sullivan points out in her study of the theology of the Council, *The Road to Vatican II*:

> Gems from the Treasure Box #1
>
>
>
> The earthly man already lives in eternity. The true state of affairs is not that this fleeting, temporal existence with all its decisions is a pure here-and-now, followed by the reward or punishment of an eternal beyond as a second existence. Rather, the two are one; one is the reverse side of the other: time is concealed eternity, and eternity is revealed time.
>
> Hans Urs von Balthasar,
> *The Grain of Wheat*

This separation between grace and nature had serious repercussions for believers in the decades before Vatican II. We could simply never be good enough, we could never "be perfect as our heavenly Father was perfect". This great gap between God and us (as we perceived it) led to a great deal of guilt and frustration. And, when you view grace as a "thing" you can get it also becomes a "thing" you can lose. Hence, we came to believe that we could "lose" God as a result of serious sin. [8]

When my father died in 2010, I remember spending an afternoon in his room after the funeral looking through his books. When he was eleven he left home to go to junior seminary in the north of Scotland to study for the priesthood. This explains the small black book I found in his collection with the title *Breviary of Piety for Clerics*. In a neat hand at the front is the inscription: "From Mother and Father to Frankie on his 14th birthday. May God bless you and bring you to his sacred altar." They never saw their son come to the altar as a priest since he left the following year, a decision that I think haunted him for the rest of his life.

The book itself is a window into the Church we have been describing, with a focus on the sacramental life, prayers and devotions. Without the flourishes of Dante, there is much detail on the fate of those who died in mortal sin and long pious descriptions of the physical sufferings Jesus endured for our sake. There's very little on the rest of the Gospel, however, which is summed up in two pages as "The Public Life of Jesus Christ". For my fourteen-year-old father, in the dark days of 1944 there was much emphasis on the pursuit of perfection, catechism and observance: this is what made you Catholic. It is also what practically guaranteed a lifelong struggle with guilt, since who among us is perfect?

It should be said that there were great benefits in belonging to what is sometimes called a "totally Catholic culture" even when, as in my own experience, it was a subculture within a ruling non-Catholic culture. This only made us stronger. It was us against the world and the world was Protestant. We had our own schools, our own clubs, our own traditions and our own language. The culture was "transmitted" by a powerful triangle of influence in the home, the school and the parish. We grew up with a strong sense of the divine, the mystical, the heroic – the world was more than it seemed. We were formed in a "sacramental imagination". Catholics loved their world, their Church. They were fiercely loyal, as minority groups often are to their tribal identity, or to use the word I often heard when growing up; they were "staunch". Many may have been suspended in a state of spiritual childhood, many were scarred by guilt and shame, but there was nevertheless a great deal of affection for the wisdom and ways of Mother Church.

There was security in such a culture. There was identity in being a cultural Catholic. You even had your own football team to support and a football team to hate. But that culture, at least in the West, has all but collapsed in the last fifty years. We are now facing what is sometimes called a "crisis of transmission" as the parishes search in vain for priests, parishioners drift away, families fracture and staff and students in Catholic schools have a much less confident grasp of the Catholic culture we once took for granted. The secular world grows in prosperity and success and looks to provide itself with entertainment and comfort. The Church is seen as marginal, a remnant, the occasional plaything of the sparkling intellectuals. Cultural Catholicism has cracked and is crumbling.

I do not believe there is any point in trying to recover the culture, since it is probably irretrievably lost. Our task as I see it is not to determine how we can survive and thrive as a holy few in the toxic wasteland of modernity, although for some that is an attractive option. Our task is to go back to our best resource in recent years – Vatican II – and use that as our road map if we wish to continue the journey towards thriving in a very different kind of Church. And it will be different. We will need to give a better account of ourselves, but the good news is there will be less guilt and fear. One of the many remarkable points to note about Vatican II is that, after all the talk of hell over the years, it is not mentioned in the documents of the Council. Professor Gavin D'Costa, writing in *The Tablet*, comments:

> Vatican II does not contain a single reference to hell even when speaking of eschatology. Karl Rahner claimed that the most significant teaching of the Council was its "salvation optimism". *Lumen Gentium*, the Council's decree on the Church, was the key. It overturned centuries of salvation pessimism: all non-Catholics… could be saved if they were ignorant of the Gospel and they sought God, or the truth, in their conscience. This was a dramatic development of doctrine.[9]

This is not to say that hell has suddenly been decommissioned, but it is an acknowledgement that it was perhaps not the best way to portray eternal separation from a loving God, which still needs to remain as an option. There will always be those who like the crackling sound of eternal damnation and we should not assume we have heard our last fiery sermon about hell, but the imaginative landscape has changed. What the Church seemed to be trying to say for all those years was that there is an urgency about your life and you have one precious chance to respond to the call of God. Since we were largely treated like children, and this thinking really took hold in the Middle Ages, it is not surprising that threats were used more than persuasion.

The Light of the World

The story of *Lumen Gentium*, one of the four constitutions of Vatican II, is a vivid illustration of the Church's remarkable journey in the last sixty years. The first draft of the document was presented to the first session of the Council in 1962. It had been written by Vatican insiders, the "company men" whose role was to maintain and defend the status quo. As Edward Hahnenberg points out, "the draft was marked by the defensive preoccupation with church structures that had shaped official church teaching since the reformation."[10] It was roundly condemned from the floor of the Council, with Bishop Emil Josef De Smedt from Belgium leading the charge. He accused the draft of triumphalism (the Church is the best) clericalism (priests and the pope are more important than anybody else) and juridicalism (the spiritual life is all about rules). The document was sent back to be radically redrafted. What emerged was a quite different vision of the Church and its people. In his moment of inspiration, Angelo Roncalli somehow sensed that beneath the serene façade of the Church in 1959, there was after all a burning desire for change.

The documents of Vatican II take their names from the initial words of the Latin text. *Lumen Gentium* ("the light of the world") puts the Church in its place in the first sentence. It is Christ who is the light of the world. The Church is there to reflect that light, as the moon reflects the light of the sun. There is no sign of the triumphalist language of the past when it comes to describing the Church, instead there is a marked humility. The Church, or "little flock of Christ", is not the kingdom of God but only the "seed and the beginning of the kingdom on earth".[11] The Church is described not in juridical, theological or legal language, but in a series of metaphors drawn from the rich tradition of biblical revelation.

The authors make the point that this was how Jesus spoke. We will look in more detail at the language of Jesus in the next chapter, but for now it is worth underlining the point that describing the Church in metaphors is an open-ended invitation to explore, examine and discuss, since metaphors by their very nature resist simplistic interpretation, as well as juridical definition. In Article 6 the Church is described as sheepfold, estate or field, building, family, temple and mother. It is also described as a bride, which is an image the Church has downplayed in recent years, given the less than spotless behaviour of some of its members.

The Council of Trent insisted that there was no salvation outside of the Church – extra Ecclesiam nulla salus. I was brought up with this belief. If you weren't a Catholic you were in very serious danger of being on the wrong side of the last judgement. Lumen Gentium changed that thinking. In fact one little Latin word changed all that. In the earlier draft it stated that the Church of Christ is ("est" in Latin) the Catholic Church. In the final draft "est" was replaced with "subsistit in". The Church "subsists in the Catholic Church… although outside its structure many elements of sanctification and of truth are to be found" (Article 8). Later in the same article there is the famous formulation regarding those who, through no fault of their own, do not know anything about Christ or his Church, "yet who search for God with a sincere heart and, under the influence of grace, try to put into effect the will of God as known to them through the dictate of conscience: these too can obtain eternal salvation" (Article 8).

Readers of a certain age may respond to this with something of a shrug (see Wendy's comment below about not having any baggage) as if to say: "What's the big deal?" But at the time it was a very big deal. Centuries of defensive, exclusive, arrogant thinking were reversed almost overnight. I well remember the confusion in the little study group my father convened in our council house in the 1970s (he had swapped his *Breviary of Piety for Clerics* for the *Documents of Vatican II*). "So what happened to mortal sin?" they would ask; or "what's the point of being a Catholic if we can all get to heaven?" These were not flippant questions. That first generation really struggled with change. What perhaps helped them was the very clear focus throughout the documents on the essentials of the Christian life.

We will look in more detail later on at what *Lumen Gentium* had to say about the laity, but on the fundamentals of the Christian life it was very clear. In place of endless clauses and formulations to remember by heart was an invitation to focus on the "soul of the apostolate" which is defined as "love for God and for people", nourished by the sacraments, especially the sacred Eucharist (Article 33). There was an unequivocal call for a "more equitable distribution" of the goods of creation (Article 36), and above all a call back to the Gospel, especially the core teaching of Jesus for "the world cannot be transformed and offered to God without the spirit of the beatitudes" (Article 31). There was, despite the discomfort of the "transitional" generation who knew both the old Church and the new, a great deal of excitement following Vatican II. Mass was heard for the first time in centuries in the local language, the priest turned to face the people, guitars replaced the organ, the historical study of the scriptures was permitted and encouraged, dialogue with other faiths got under way, lay people became involved in parish life. It was a kind of springtime.

It is beyond the scope of this book to look in any detail at the period of church history defined by the papacies of Saint John Paul II and Benedict XVI, but for some these were years when the reforms of Vatican II slowed down and during the pontificate of Benedict seemed to go into reverse (see Greg's comments at the end of the chapter on this point). The traditionalists were in clover, the liberals were in despair. But we must also try and understand the situation faced by these popes. They were both men of huge intellect and deep faith, brought up in their own "totally Catholic cultures", but exposed in their formative years to ideologies to which the word "evil" could be applied without hesitation. They were also greatly concerned by the pace of secularisation which the fathers of Vatican II were just beginning to understand. For them I believe there was very good reason to focus once more on authority, unity and the enduring teaching of the Catholic Church.

It did not help of course that during the final years of Benedict's reign the Church was assailed by wave after wave of revelations of child abuse scandals. It is also now clear that during the final years of the publicly ailing John Paul II, very little was done to combat the culture of the "company men" in the Vatican Curia, who had never gone away. The time was ripe for another moment of inspiration and it was delivered in a very similar style to Angelo Roncalli's announcement of Vatican II. In a routine statement to a group of cardinals on 11 February 2013, Benedict XVI said that he would be retiring as pope. He spoke in Latin and it is said that not everyone in the room understood right away what he had said. Apparently one or two cardinals exchanged nervous glances, as if to say: "Did you just hear what I heard?"

A pope had not resigned since Gregory XII in 1415. This was huge. The official reason given by Benedict is that he was getting too old for the job, but rumours continue to this day that he had had enough of the decadent culture of the Curia, the Vatican's government, which was generating its own scandals. It was a brave and bold decision. Just over two months later, one Jorge Mario Bergoglio ("Who?", many asked) emerged on to the balcony of Saint Peter's as the new pope and with disarming informality said to the assembled thousands and the millions watching at home: "Brothers and sisters, good evening." Before he blessed the assembly in the square he asked them to bless him and bowed before them in silence. Once again, something quite extraordinary was taking place. Cardinal Walter Kasper is in no doubt that Francis was chosen for a reason: "Francis was elected Pope in order to lead the church out of the crisis that came to light in the Vatileaks and other scandals. A missionary church, as Francis understands it, must be a church that takes the path of renewal."[12]

In a few short months Pope Francis touched the hearts of millions across the world not so much with words but with actions. His patron, Saint Francis, is supposed to have said: "Preach the gospel and use words if you have to." The first *magisterium* (teaching) authority of Francis was choosing not to live in the papal apartments, washing the feet of juvenile delinquents (male and female, which was against the "rules"), the public embrace of a deformed man and his decision to invite three homeless men to celebrate his seventy-seventh birthday by joining him for breakfast. His first written publication, apostolic exhortation *Evangelii Gaudium* ("The Joy of the Gospel"),[13] is like nothing any pope has ever published before in terms of its urgency, tone and candour.

Like every other papal publication, however, it does seem to be taking its time getting through to ordinary lay people in the Church, let alone those on the outside looking in. When I attended an evening of musical worship at a local parish, the lead singer asked the congregation if they had read *Evangelii Gaudium*. Two hands went up in a crowded church (one of them was mine). This is probably a hangover from the culture in which only the clergy and academics read church documents, but that has to change. We really need to get reading, get studying. I know the latest papal exhortation is not essential for the Christian life but something very profound is again stirring in the Church, and for anyone on the way out this one could be a lifeline; for anybody on the threshold it is a powerful invitation; and for those inside I would suggest it is required reading as we seek to give some direction to the people of God in the early twenty-first century.

In language strikingly reminiscent of John XXIII's opening address to Vatican II, Francis says in *Evangelii Gaudium*: "Rather than experts in dire predictions, dour judges bent on rooting out every threat and deviation, we should appear as joyful messengers of challenging proposals, guardians of the goodness and beauty which shine forth in a life of fidelity to the Gospel" (Article 13). He calls us back to the source, the reason we call ourselves Christians. As John XXIII did, he calls for a fraternal engagement with the modern world and a creative and personal commitment to "the original freshness of the Gospel". Being a Catholic, he implies, is not about following a thousand rules. In fact, in what sounds like a rebuke to that mindset, he calls us to "concentrate on the essentials, on what is most beautiful, most grand, most appealing and at the same time most necessary" (Article 35). It is not so much a call to be a Catholic but a call to be a Christian, to be a disciple. And for any tired-out, would-be or sort-of disciple there is really only one place to start: Jesus Christ.

Gems from the Treasure Box #2

The ordinary is only a problem in a de-sacralised world in which the secular refuses to be graced. The theology of grace that informs Vatican II recovers "the ordinary" as the realm of grace, God's "better beauty", hence the aesthetic of holiness is not something exceptional but something that is shaped in the realm of the domestic, giving to it the weight of glory.

Heythrop Institute for Religion, *Ethics and Public Life, On the Way to Life*

Jesus of Nazareth

My first image of Jesus was a picture of the Sacred Heart which hung on the wall at the foot of my bed. Jesus opened his chest to reveal a heart blazing out with love for the human race. One stormy night I was convinced that the lips were moving and a real light was shining from the chest cavity. My next image of Jesus was a small white host at the far end of the church which the priest held up at Mass. That too was Jesus, I was told. There was also a statue of a child dressed up as a little prince in the front room, Jesus as the Child of Prague. Some have seen this image as a clever ruse dreamt up by European monarchy to equate obedience to them with obedience to Jesus. These were some of the images of Jesus I inherited from my Catholic culture.

Experts would no doubt be able to explain the psychological damage such images may have inflicted but I have survived to tell the tale. I did not, however, have much of a notion well into adulthood about who Jesus was and how he might have anything to do with my life. That's quite an admission from someone who called himself a "practising Catholic" at job interviews, but I have to say it is the truth. I am a practising Catholic (hopefully in a deeper sense than just attendance at Mass) but for much of my life Jesus seemed a remotely tortured figure or else a glorious presence high above the human fray. That was the experience of many people.

Jesus was often taught as one "topic" among many in the impressively complex Catechism which had developed over the years. Sherry Weddell illustrates the point with an anecdote which will resonate with many:

> I once helped design an RCIA [Rite of Christian Initiation for Adults] program with a group of friends. We thought it would be valuable and fun to let the group encounter Jesus directly by reading the Gospel of Luke together during inquiry. The director of religious education disapproved and told us we were "too Christocentric". Whenever we treat Jesus as a "topic" within the faith instead of as the "whole spiritual good of the Church" [*Catechism of the Catholic Church*, 1324]… we profoundly distort the faith and communicate an impersonal or institutional understanding of what it means to be Catholic.[14]

The Council fathers attempted to wipe away the dust of such pedagogy and declared in no uncertain terms that Jesus Christ was the central "topic" – the first and the last, Alpha and Omega. Earlier in this chapter, we saw the best example of this in the resounding opening words of *Lumen Gentium*, "Christ is the light of the world." The point is made with great clarity and emphasis by Blessed Pope Paul VI, who became pope after the death of John XXII in 1963 and steered the Council through to its conclusion: "There is no true evangelization if the name, the teaching, the life, the promises, the kingdom and the mystery of Jesus of Nazareth, the Son of God, are not proclaimed."[15]

Comments from the twelve on a "totally Catholic culture", Vatican II and Pope Francis

Pope Francis has brought, for me, a reminder that the Church is not made up only of doctrine and liturgy. In one sense John Paul II was very much concerned with doctrine, as was Benedict with liturgy. So what Francis brings is that reminder of the Catholic nature of the Church; it's made up of many dimensions. So it is two particular charisms that seem to just pulse through his ministry. The first one is about the poor and that social sensitivity that you can't follow the Gospel, you can't do liturgy perfectly, you can't have all the right doctrinal thoughts and ignore poverty, pain and suffering, both within the Church and outside the Church. Number two: he's brought in this theme, which is totally unresolved, of mercy and charity and we're seeing that right now in the whole synod of the family, this kind of incredible moment of thinking "how do we remain faithful to doctrine and how do we act on that doctrine so that it actually exemplifies an open and welcoming Church?"

In that sense it's a kind of Catholic moment, the history of the popes is always this, you have one who's absolutely obsessed with reforming the calendar, another who wants to reform Canon Law etc. So if you look at them on their own they all have little obsessions but what's wonderful is if you look at them together they form some composite picture which gives us hope and I would say this is the case. So what he's brought in first is this sense in which doctrine and liturgy, without social action and attention, both within and outside the Church, is actually not the Gospel.

Greg, 56, university teacher

One of the most fascinating things for me is that here you have an institution of the papacy which is always portrayed, and part of its own self-portrayal, as stable and unchanging. Yet look at how often it has surprised us. It has surprised us in John XXIII calling a council, it's surprised us in the extraordinary leadership, I think, of Paul VI, but then choosing a Polish pope, choosing a German pope and then in choosing a Jesuit Latin American pope? That doesn't seem to me to be a conservative institution. That seems to be an extraordinary institution and also a sign of deep vitality and the movement of the Spirit within the Church.

I would see all of that in terms of the event of the Council and I suppose another way of looking at it is when you have an event it doesn't cease, the moment may cease, as it did in 1965, but the event carries on and I think we're still living it. In a sense the Council remains unfinished because the Church is still going on developing, writing, living. So in that sense I think hermeneutically you can say it's an extraordinary moment and therefore I think that we can trust it because I think it is genuinely the action of the Holy Spirit.

James, 64, religious order

Some of my frustration about actually trying to be a Catholic has been when other people don't seem to understand Vatican II. You still discover things in Catholicism that make you think "that's not what we believe" and I think it is because people haven't moved into Vatican II. Very hierarchical priesthood – that's not what Vatican II says. Fear of the world – that's not what Vatican II says. Openness to transforming culture is what Vatican II tells us to do. It talks about the laity as partners but not in the sense of being the same as Father but in the sense of dignity and mission in the world. So for me, what was my formation in Catholicism? It was reading Vatican II and fortunately [as a convert] I didn't have any of the other baggage to get shot of.

Wendy, 52, teacher

There was a very good debate between an American Catholic theologian and a member of one of these right-wing splinter groups, all about whether or not Vatican II was genuine. Of course these guys would say that Satan basically infiltrated the Vatican and managed to convince all the bishops to go along with all this stuff and break with tradition. It wasn't that either, of course not. So it was a wonderful thing, it is, to quote Robert Barron "an evolution, not a revolution". There are some good videos on YouTube where he talks about Vatican II actually, if you're interested. I haven't read the documents as such but it's on my list of things to read this year.

Paul, 23, chaplaincy assistant

I don't think I could ever answer every single question on the Catechism but it was a thorough training. I went to a Jesuit school and that was a very, very thorough Catholic education. It had the effect of feeling that literally the Catholic world was complete. At the end of the religious lesson, the Jesuit priests would have a kind of question-and-answer session. You could throw anything at all at them and of course they'd heard it all before and they answered very easily. Some days we felt we were given the answer that would satisfy a teenager, they wouldn't actually give you the full answer that would satisfy them, but one still had the impression that from a rational point of view the faith was something complete.

Tom, 78, retired schoolmaster

I grew up with memorising all the prayers, some I did not understand because they were in Latin and I think some were in Filipino which were quite deep in relation to the language, so I had difficulty with that. Somehow the rituals that I went through grounded me or it made me appreciate that there's a God and there's always the presence that is always there to help you out. Initially it was really just saying, "I need this. I need this. Help me, help me", but as I went through journeying, because I am journeying with people, with theologians etc., somehow I found some rituals that I don't do as much as before or I don't go into memorising prayers and it's more appreciating, like I find God in nature.

When we're in the farm I appreciate so much when it rains and you see the beauty of the environment and it's not something that is just there, it was given to you. I always find comfort in knowing, especially if you have difficult times, that this thing is not given to me for nothing. My God is not giving me a hard time. There's something good in it. It's something that is offered to me and I can see the goodness in what is being given or what is being presented. There's a tendency for many of us to be very demanding: "This is what I need", "Why am I going through this?" But sometimes it seems as if there are problems but they're not really problems.

Rebecca, 51, Dean of Studies

Reflections **for individuals**

- In your journal write down your own experience of the institutional Church, either from within or without, from childhood to adulthood. How do you see the Church today?

- Read *Evangelii Gaudium* by Pope Francis (take your time, it is a long and rich document). What strikes you about the message and how it is presented? Perhaps write out your favourite quotations in your journal.

- How do you respond to the reflections from some of the twelve (above)? Do any of them strike a chord with you?

Reflection **activity for groups**

- Read Articles 4-6 of *Lumen Gentium*. Which metaphors for the Church do you find most attractive and why? Choose one and open out the wider interpretations of the image.

- On a flipchart or large piece of paper write "The Church" in the centre, then brainstorm everyone's response to that word. Spend some time in discussion about what people come up with. What kind of view of the Church does it give you? How broad is the understanding of Church, how positive or negative, what images or metaphors are used? What does it tell you about your own community?

Resources for further study

Walter Abbott SJ (ed.), *The Documents of Vatican II* (London: Chapman, 1966). The first collection to be published in English of the sixteen official texts promulgated by the Council. It is probably only available second-hand but is worth tracking down – a wonderful resource with excellent introductory essays by those who were very close to the Council. This was among my father's books.

Edward Hahnenberg, *A Concise Guide to the Documents of Vatican II* (Cincinnati: Franciscan Media, 2007). An ideal book for those who want a helpful introduction and background to each of the sixteen documents.

Maureen Sullivan OP, *The Road to Vatican II: Key Changes in Theology* (New York: Paulist Press, 2007). For those who want a bit more background to the theology of the Council this lucid and engaging book is well worthwhile.

Avery Dulles, *Models of the Church* (New York: Doubleday, 2002). This is something of a classic work for those who want to explore further the idea of models of the Church. This was another title among my father's books.

Notes

[1] Pope Saint John XXIII, Opening Address to the Second Vatican Council, http://www.catholicculture.org/culture/library/view.cfm?RecNum=3233, accessed 20 October 2014

[2] E.P. Hahnenberg, *A Concise Guide to the Documents of Vatican II* (Cincinnati: Franciscan Media, 2007), 2

[3] John XXIII, Opening Address to the Second Vatican Council.

[4] Hahnenberg, *Concise Guide*, 5

[5] Pope Pius IX, *The Syllabus of Errors*, http://www.papalencyclicals.net/Pius09/p9syll.htm, accessed 20 October 2014

[6] G.W. Hughes SJ, *God of Surprises* (London: Darton, Longman & Todd, 1985), 19

[7] Dante, *The Divine Comedy: Hell*, trans. Dorothy L. Sayers (London: Penguin, 1949), 286

[8] M. Sullivan OP, *The Road to Vatican II: Key Changes in Theology* (New York: Paulist Press, 2007), 48

[9] G. D'Costa, "Who Gets In, and Who is Kept Out" (*The Tablet*, 3 February 2013)

[10] Hahnenberg, *Concise Guide*, 39

[11] Second Vatican Council, *Lumen Gentium* (Dogmatic Constitution on the Church), 4. http://www.vatican.va/archive/hist_councils/ii_vatican_council/documents/vat-ii_const_19641121_lumen-gentium_en.html, accessed 24 July 2015

[12] Cardinal Walter Kasper, *Pope Francis' Revolution of Tenderness and Love* (New York: Paulist Press, 2015), 47

[13] Pope Francis, *Evangelii Gaudium* (The Joy of the Gospel), 168. http://w2.vatican.va/content/francesco/en/apost_exhortations/documents/papa-francesco_esortazione-ap_20131124_evangelii-gaudium.html, accessed 24 July 2015

[14] Sherry A. Weddell, *Forming Intentional Disciples* (Huntington: Our Sunday Visitor, 2012), 143

[15] Pope Paul VI, *Evangelii Nuntiandi* (Evangelization in the Modern World), 22 http://w2.vatican.va/content/paul-vi/en/apost_exhortations/documents/hf_p-vi_exh_19751208_evangelii-nuntiandi.html

"What are you looking for?" – Jesus in the Gospels

Catholics had not heard the Gospel of Jesus of Nazareth for many years. At Mass the readings were in Latin, which meant that most of the congregation did not understand a word. The sermons often had little to do with the Gospel and although they weren't always the fire-and-brimstone variety of James Joyce there was a good deal of existential threat behind the moral instruction. That was about to change. The Council decreed that "easy access to holy scripture should be available to all the Christian faithful". [1] The people would hear the Word of God in their own language, as the reformers had been advocating for hundreds of years.

Moreover, the Council was determined that the laity would benefit from the many years of Protestant scholarship which had made such progress in understanding how the Bible was written. In the mainstream Catholic Church there was little knowledge of the context in which the biblical texts were produced. In 1964, the Pontifical Biblical Commission published a short document entitled *Instruction on the Historical Truth of the Gospels*, which informed *Dei Verbum*, the Council's Constitution on Divine Revelation quoted above. In the *Instruction* Catholic scholars were given permission to follow the "historical method" which allowed them to investigate the historical context in which the scriptures were written, while always doing so in the light of faith. The *Instruction* outlines three stages in the development of the Gospels.

Stage 1 is the public ministry of Jesus. In that period of approximately three years (some say less) nothing was recorded about what Jesus did or said.

Stage 2 is the oral transmission and preaching by the apostles following the death and resurrection of Jesus. These were the eyewitnesses to the events of the public ministry. Again, nothing was written down for perhaps four decades (apart from Paul's letters written in the AD 50s) and what may have been written was lost. The memory was transmitted orally and what they said developed over time as their faith matured and was shaped by their context. They were not simply transmitting a fixed memory.

Stage 3 is the actual composition of the Gospels by evangelists who were almost certainly not eyewitnesses, but who relied on key witnesses and drew on the oral tradition and then "selected certain things out of the many which had been handed on; some they synthesised, some they explained with an eye to the situation of the churches".[2] The eminent Catholic scripture scholar Raymond E. Brown estimates the Gospels were written in a period from c. AD 70–90, "fixing Mark about 70, Matthew and Luke in the period 80–90 and John in the 90s".[3] He adds that there may have been some written material from the Jesus tradition already in existence before the evangelists composed their Gospels but none of that material is preserved for us.

In our time, it is like recalling the events around the death of American President John F. Kennedy in 1963. That is the kind of distance from us the Gospels were from the death of Jesus. Not only that, but imagine the death of JFK with no recorded accounts: no shaky film footage, no recorded interviews on the scene, no press coverage, just the oral testimony of those who were close to the President (and they weren't all there when he died), passed on and preserved for five decades before four people who were not eyewitnesses, living in four very different communities, decided to write an account. The four accounts would all be shaped by and directed to the communities who would hear them. There may be some aspects of the President's life and thoughts which would inspire or comfort their particular community given the challenges they faced.

Many scholars believe that Mark wrote his Gospel for the Christian community in Rome around AD 70, at a time when they were suffering persecution under the Emperor Nero. Some historians say that Christians turned on other Christians, handing them over to the authorities. It was a time of the midnight thud on the door, the scurry of arrests and betrayals, degrading imprisonment followed by public and pitiful execution. Luke probably wrote his Gospel for a community which contained a high number of poor people, possibly slaves, while Matthew seemed to be writing for a more established and comfortable community with a strong Jewish presence. John on the other hand, writing perhaps sixty years after Stage 1, was dealing with an even more developed theology and an acrimonious final split between the emerging Christian community and the Jewish synagogue.

This historical method is not intended to challenge the faith or assumptions of anybody on the threshold of discipleship, but to act as an invitation to a richly human but divinely inspired story. The Gospels are not pious collections of sayings that are interchangeable but four very different versions of the remarkable ministry of Jesus: the story of how God – the holy mystery – chose to reveal himself to humankind in the person of a first-century provincial Jew. After many years of a quiet country life, and then a period of time with his mentor John the Baptist, Jesus of Nazareth started to preach about God's order and call some people to follow him. For today's disciples (or those thinking about it) it is interesting to note the different nature of the calls. In Mark's Gospel, everything is urgent. Jesus calls and the apostles drop their nets and follow him. It is almost hypnotic and not very true to life. It may be a reflection of the urgency of his Roman community: you're either a disciple or you're not.

Come and see

In Luke, with the call of Simon Peter, there is more drama. It is clear that Jesus already knows Simon. He has spent some time at Capernaum, has healed Simon's mother-in-law and is highly thought of for his authority and power. It is interesting to note that he has been rejected at this stage by the good people of Nazareth who cannot cope with his new identity as a prophet: "Is not this Joseph's son?" (Luke 4:22). It seems to be a feature of discipleship that not all those who are called can go back to their previous lives, which can be a painful separation. Jesus is preaching in the shallows of the lake from Simon's boat and once he has finished preaching he says to Simon: "Put out into the deep water and let your nets down for a catch" (Luke 5:4). It is an invitation to let go, to emerge from the shallows of smallness and embark on a disciple's journey of depth and danger. Peter does what he is told and makes a miraculous catch of fish. He now knows that this path is divinely sanctioned, which is what scares the hell out of him.

His response, as so often with Peter, is very human and reassuring for those maybe-disciples who keep backing off when they get near some sort of step of faith: "Go away from me, Lord, for I am a sinful man!" (Luke 5:8). He cannot cope with this new identity. He considers himself, as many of us do after years of training in the art of self-reproach, as not worthy. Jesus is clearly not too worried about worthiness. He does not have a very rigorous selection process for his top team. His main purpose is to calm them down. So many of us suffer from anxiety, we worry about many things, we cannot see the way clear to make any kind of faith commitment because of the thousand obstacles we put in our way; mostly our own inadequate sense of ourselves. Jesus is happy to work with the bundle of self-loathing we now call the first pope: "Do not be afraid; from now on you will be catching people" (Luke 5:10).

In John, we find a situation that seems quite modern, as if in his community there's more time to think about your options. In Chapter 1, John the Baptist points Jesus out to two of his disciples and says: "Look, here is the Lamb of God!" (John 1:36). The disciples follow after Jesus and he turns to them and utters a phrase which must resonate with all those who are searching for meaning: "What are you looking for?" (1:38). The disciples do not reply with a long list of philosophical questions, but rather: "Where are you staying?" (1:38). Jesus then extends the invitation to those on the threshold in every generation: "Come and see" (1:39). They spend the day with him and as if the experience is so strongly marked on their memory they mention the time of day, "about four o'clock in the afternoon" (1:39).

What did they talk about all day? I can't imagine Jesus lecturing them for eight hours; that's not consistent with that initial exchange of dialogue. I can only imagine a *conversation*, which is probably not the kind of God we were expecting. God walks among us and wants to talk to us. He reveals himself in friendship, in human language, in patient dialogue, as we'll see later when we consider the conversation with the woman at the well. With these initial questions Jesus indicates the first step in discipleship: looking for something else, something more. There is perhaps a sense of deficit, a nagging feeling that there has to be more to life than this. Denis McBride, in *Jesus and the Gospels*, describes this stage as "dissatisfaction".[4]

For those who choose to move on and do something about it the next stage is often a fascination with a person or idea that might answer the dissatisfaction. Many people in the Gospels were fascinated by Jesus. There was something very different about this preacher from Galilee. He taught "with authority" (Mark 1:22) and performed miracles. The modern mind is often very sceptical about miracles, and that includes many modern Catholics, but Raymond E. Brown comments that "one of the oldest memories of him may have been that he did wondrous things". Brown also reminds us that the Jewish historian Josephus, writing in the AD 90s, described Jesus as a "doer of wonderful deeds".[5] Jesus did say, of course, that the miracles were not really the point. It was the inner healing that was more important. No wonder people were fascinated.

But fascination is not the same as discipleship. You can be fascinated by charisma, wonderful deeds, authority, and then go home at the end of the day and tell the family all about it, as if you've just seen a great movie. Many people in the Gospels were "astounded" (Luke 4:32) by Jesus but did not feel any further desire to engage or be claimed by this wandering teacher. It is when we are attracted by what fascinates us that that the fascination moves to "desire", the next stage:

> When we feel that desire we become apprentices and try to attach ourselves to the person who inspired us. We want to make the original experience a part of our lives. What we have seen and heard is no longer something to admire from a distance, it is now something to participate in, a new life that we want to share in ourselves. We do not walk away or go home; we *follow* what we find fascinating.[6]

Gerard W. Hughes makes the same point when he says that: "If God is not attractive to us, then we cannot desire him."[7] Why would we fall in love with a God who wanted to torture us forever if we got it wrong? How could we fall in love with anyone who *made* us follow them? Why would we follow a God-man who burdened us with misery and guilt? Those who follow Jesus do not find themselves in thrall to some guru figure who keeps them in a state of dependence on his power. In John's Gospel, he calls his disciples "friends" (John 15:15). He points away from himself all the time. Many people who encountered him, especially the band of hostile clerics who seemed to haunt his every step, wanted to know by what authority he acted and spoke. Jesus never claims to be the origin of the power he shows in his public life: "But if it is by the finger of God that I cast out the demons, then the kingdom of God has come to you" (Luke 11:20). He constantly seeks to foster the growth of his disciples so that they will find the confidence to pass the message on.

In Chapter 1, we described a Catholic community in which membership was inherited and sustained by cultural support and assent to a body of belief. This produced Catholics, but it did not always produce Christians. It certainly produced very few who were familiar with the scriptures. In fact those who got excited about the Gospel in adulthood were often considered as taking things a bit far, becoming a bit *evangelical*. That was very much the "folk" Church of mass membership. The Church of the twenty-first century, at least in the West, does not look as if it will resemble that. That is not to say that doctrine will be diluted or made easier, but the initial movement to follow Jesus Christ will probably not come from a conviction that all these doctrines are the answer to my life's questions, but from some kind of personal encounter with him. This is what people are looking for and one of the biggest reasons they give for leaving the Church is the absence of such an encounter.

My interviews with the twelve were as interesting for what they didn't say as for what they said. Mostly they were embarrassed or reluctant to talk about their own faith commitment or calling, a phenomenon I have never experienced among evangelical Christians whose stories of being called or "born again" are central to their discipleship. For most cradle Catholics there is no blinding flash on the road to Damascus which throws them to the ground in shock and awe. It does of course happen, as Greg testifies, but for most it is a long and winding road. My own experience was very much the path of the cradle Catholic, brought up in a supportive Catholic culture: home, school, and parish all working together to provide a kind of catechesis by osmosis. It was the air we breathed.

I did feel called to another level of discipleship when I was ten. I told my parents that I wanted to go to junior seminary to be a priest, just as my father had done thirty years before. I even ended up in the same seminary in the north of Scotland. What attracted me to this calling? Was it Jesus, or some human proxy? To disentangle the entire psychology of a personal calling is probably best kept for the memoirs but it was certainly a combination of assumed parental expectation (although it was never made explicit), the charisma of our post-Vatican II guitar-wielding priest, some fear of the rough secondary school I was due to attend, and a sense of adventure and heroic service handed down from the lives of the saints. (Through all of that of course is the prompting of the Spirit, but that is beyond analysis.) I stayed in the seminary until I was nineteen, having studied at a senior seminary in Ireland for two years, and left for much the same reason described by Greg. It wasn't for me, but there was something bugging me which kept me connected to the wandering path of discipleship. I felt somehow that I was close to the truth of things and that was where I needed to be. As the years have gone on I am deeply grateful that I hung in there and tried to grow in my faith, above all in recent years by discovering Jesus and the Gospels.

Gems from the Treasure Box #3

Conversion is like stepping across the chimneypiece out of a Looking-Glass world, where everything is an absurd caricature, into the real world God made; and then begins the delicious process of exploring it limitlessly.

Evelyn Waugh,
Letter to Edward Sackville-West

But I say to you

Jesus did not leave us with a catechism, or any written body of carefully constructed religious instruction. He did not write anything or ask anyone else to write anything down as far as we know. To the mind of God it seemed that the revelation of his nature would be better served within the human limitations of memory and the struggle for understanding. We have to assume that God could have ordered revelation otherwise, he could have provided a complete "download" that answered every question and covered every base. But what he left us with were stories, sayings and deeds that were held in the memory of a small number of people until the time came to write them down. It is there we must look to find Jesus and what he revealed about God.

In the previous chapter we saw the prominence which *Lumen Gentium* gave to the beatitudes. In Christian thinking, this collection of teaching from Matthew and Luke's Gospel is often seen as the essence, the core of the teaching of Jesus. The Catechism is unequivocal about their centrality: "The beatitudes are at the heart of Jesus' preaching… They depict the very countenance of Jesus and they characterise authentic Christian life."[8] But there is more than one version. The differences between them are a perfect illustration of the complexities of Stage 3 of the composition process. For years Matthew's Gospel was given prominence in the Church as the "teaching" Gospel. He had a genius for ordering his material in ways which helped catechists through the ages. His beatitudes are delivered by Jesus "up the mountain" (Matthew 5:1) and seemingly only to the twelve. Matthew is more formal in his style and tone than Luke. The community he was writing for, perhaps in Antioch, had people who were materially comfortable. He does not castigate the rich. Matthew's beatitudes begin with: "Blessed are the poor *in spirit*" (5:3).

Luke's beatitudes are delivered "on a level place" (6:17) and seemingly to a wider group of disciples. In his community, perhaps on the Greek mainland, there were poor people and slaves. His version of the beatitudes begins: "Blessed are you who are poor" (6:20). He means the actual poor, not the comfortable people who have a humble spirit. Both accounts of the beatitudes go on to spell out a series of counter-cultural instructions: "You have heard that it was said… But I say to you…" (Matthew 5:21-22). This was not, and is still not, conventional human wisdom but it is the wisdom of God's order, God's reign, or God's kingdom. As Saint Paul says, in a poignant phrase from his first letter to the Corinthians, "None of the rulers of this age understood this; for if they had, they would not have crucified the Lord of glory" (1 Corinthians 2:8).

In his recorded talks on the Gospel of Luke[9] Raymond E. Brown comments on the importance of having different versions of the teaching of the beatitudes. The Church also has to preach to those with possessions. The Church has never said you need to give everything away before you can join (although much to our discomfort that's exactly what Jesus says in Luke's Gospel, 14:33). All four Gospels refer to Joseph of Arimathea as someone who helped to bury Jesus after the crucifixion, but only Mathew calls him "a rich man… who was also a disciple of Jesus" (27:57). In our times, however, perhaps we should be more inclined to Luke's emphasis, as Pope

Francis has tried to set a new direction for the Church. In *Evangelii Gaudium* (*EG*; "The Joy of the Gospel") he says:

> I want a church which is poor and for the poor. They have much to teach us. Not only do they share in the *sensus fidei* but in their difficulties they know the suffering Christ. We need to let ourselves be evangelised by them. [10]

The Church is seen by many as an institution of great wealth. Whether that is fair or not today, it was certainly the case for much of history. Pope Francis has issued a call for the Church to be poor and in this we have to say we are closer to our Lord. There is no evidence in any of the Gospel traditions that Jesus had possessions, craved possessions or saw them as important. In Luke's Gospel Jesus speaks of the danger of building bigger barns, storing up treasure on this earth (Luke 12: 13-21). Most of us would consider that to be no more than good business practice, or putting something aside for the family. Jesus is very sharp with the man who represents this mind-set: "You fool, this very night your life is being demanded of you! And the things you have prepared, whose will they be?" (12:20). Pope Francis, in his reading of the modern age, is deeply concerned about the corrosive effects of a "complacent and covetous heart" (*EG* 2). Those on the threshold of the Church should not worry that they will be asked to sell their car or their house, but they have to recognise the great attraction in a Lord who was completely uninterested in material gain. There is something about a devotion to *stuff* that chokes the spirit and ultimately leaves you dissatisfied. As we'll see in Chapter 6, that view is surprisingly widely held.

The kingdom of God is like

Apart from the exhortations of the beatitudes, or the sermon on the mount/plain, the favoured teaching technique of Jesus was the parable, in fact in Matthew's Gospel it says that "without a parable he told them nothing" (13:34). Like the figurative language used to describe the Church in *Lumen Gentium*, a parable is a teaching method which invites discussion, reflection, interpretation, rather than providing clear ethical instruction. (See Xita's comments at the end of this chapter on the importance of parables for her.) It is interesting to note that not many parables are quoted in official church documents. The Church we described in Chapter 1 preferred answers, clarity, resolution, but that was not the way of Jesus. Consider how often in the Gospels you hear Jesus answering a question directly. Hardly ever. Admittedly, a lot of the questions he is asked are traps so he has to be careful. But more often than not he answers questions indirectly, often with a parable.

In all of the synoptic Gospels (Mark, Matthew and Luke) the parables are a substantial part of what was handed on by the Stage 2 oral tradition. This has to tell us that they were central to the teaching method of Jesus. He rarely defines the kingdom of God in the kind of juridical language we were brought up with, but keeps using *similes*: "What is the kingdom of God like?" (Luke 13:18). In the world of the parable we are not told the answer but we are confronted with an imaginative challenge: where is the kingdom in this story; where is Jesus; where are we? In Luke's Gospel when somebody asked Jesus who is my neighbour he replied with the parable of the Good

> **Gems from the Treasure Box #4**
>
> I think that we have greatly deformed the gospel. We have tried to live a very comfortable gospel, without committing ourselves, merely being pious, having a gospel that we are content with.
>
> Blessed Oscar Romero, *Through the Year with Oscar Romero: Daily Meditations*

Samaritan (Luke 10:25-37). Who are we: the nervous priest and Levite who scuttle past the beaten-up guy on the road, because it is easier not to get involved? Or the outsider, the Samaritan, who goes out of his way to help?

It is not a story that would have been well received by the clerics in the audience. They are portrayed as indifferent to human suffering, unmerciful. There was constant conflict in the Gospels between Jesus and the religious authorities of his day. Some people consider this as inevitable since he was in the process of founding a new religion but there is very little evidence for that. Jesus was a Jew and operated within Judaism, but with a very clear challenge to a legalistic mind-set and a fiercely consistent bias for the vulnerable. McBride comments that the parable form *"subverts* the world by exposing oppression and selfishness; these stories attempt to introduce new values". That is why Jesus ended up tortured to death between two thieves, "not because he entertained people with harmless spiritual stories about the kingdom come, but because he told dangerous stories which radically challenged what was happening in the real kingdoms of his own time".[11] He holds a mirror up to his society and challenges a status quo that tolerates massive inequality, exploitation and injustice.

In Luke, for example, Jesus tells the parable of the Rich Man and Lazarus (Luke 16:19-31). The socially acceptable division between a rich man at his table and a poor man at his gate is thrown into reverse in heaven, or as McBride comments the parable "refuses to acquiesce in the quaint belief that what is tolerable in society is eternally sanctioned by God".[12] The point is not that the poor man will get his reward in heaven and the selfish man will go to hell but that this situation is not in accordance with the mind of God in the here and now. The rich should not ignore the poor, because they have influence with God. In the parables of Jesus there is a particular focus on oppressive behaviour and the way the vulnerable are treated. Matthew's Last Judgement (25:31-46) is an even less ambiguous message that the *only* thing we will be judged on is how we treated the last and the least. It makes it clear to us that in the story of the Good Samaritan the beaten-up lump on the side of the road is none other than Jesus.

Change your mind

The parables need to be seen in the wider context of the preaching and teaching of Jesus. The first message delivered by Jesus is a well-known formula to those on the threshold of discipleship: "Repent, for the kingdom of heaven has come near" (Matthew 3:2). I have spent most of my life as a Catholic thinking that meant I had to be sorry for my sins, which is actually not that difficult to do. I am sorry for my sins (at least most of them). And if I sinned again because of ingrained and inherited weakness I could always go to confession and start all over, but that is not the power of that statement.

Gerard W. Hughes, among many other scholars, points out that "repentance is the translation of a Greek word, *metanoia*, which means a change of mind and heart, a change of outlook."[13] Jesus spoke in Aramaic, not Greek, but the Greek word *metanoia* was the one chosen by the Stage 3 synoptic authors to get closest to what they thought Jesus meant by that summons. Thomas Keating, the American Trappist monk, says that: "To repent is not to take on afflictive penances like fasting, vigils, flagellation, or whatever else appeals to your generosity. It means *to change the direction in which you are looking for happiness*."[14] This might explain why Jesus had so much trouble with religious folk. When you think you have all the answers, when your mind is *set* after years of training and observance, you don't take too kindly to being told to change direction. The tax collectors and sinners didn't have much of a problem with that. They were more than ready to look somewhere else for happiness.

The perspective of Jesus can be illustrated very well by his approach to table fellowship and specifically the people he consistently chose to eat with, especially in Luke's Gospel. On one occasion, he challenges the normal etiquette when he is invited to dine at the house of a Pharisee. He notices the great attention the guests paid to the "places of honour" (Luke 14:7) which, if we are honest, is still very much part of our thinking today. Jesus does not criticise them outright but resorts to a parable about wedding guests (14:8-11) and being humble in the social order. But just in case his host hasn't quite got the point, he then spells it out: when you give a banquet, don't invite your friends. Why not? Because they will repay you and the system is maintained. What you should do when you give a banquet is "invite the poor, the crippled, the lame, and the blind, because they cannot repay you" (14:13). If the banquet is a metaphor for the bounty of God then it truly is good news.

Jesus spelled out his mission fairly clearly: "I was sent only to the lost sheep of the house of Israel" (Matthew 15:24). It seems in Luke's Gospel that one of his favourite locations to meet with the lost sheep is at table, but he does not impose any preconditions on his table fellowship. He does not say be good and pure and worthy and *then* you can sit at table with me. That was the approach of the Pharisees. For Jesus, it is the reverse. He invites them to table with him in the hope that they will experience welcome,

Gems from the Treasure Box #5

In the white blaze of this kingdom of his there was to be no property, no privilege, no pride and precedence; no motive indeed and no reward but love. Is it any wonder that men were dazzled and blinded and cried out against him? Even his disciples cried out when he would not spare them the light. Is it any wonder that the priests realized that between this man and themselves there was no choice but that he or priestcraft should perish? For to take him seriously was to enter upon a strange and alarming life, to abandon habits, to control instincts and impulses, to essay an incredible happiness.

H.G. Wells,
A Short History of the World

forgiveness, conversion, *metanoia – in that order*. McBride summarises the strategy of Jesus as follows:

> His radical belief is that unrestricted table fellowship and indiscriminate welcome are the best ways of bringing salvation to people, especially those who are excluded from the Temple or the tables of the righteous. And since he believes that the kingdom of God looks like a magnificent feast for the legion of the unwanted, Jesus displays God's unique style in the present tense. Jesus wants the unwanted; he loves the unloved; he has a passion to break bread with broken people."[15]

We can see this illustrated in the memorable story of the encounter with Zacchaeus, whom Luke makes a point of telling us was a "chief tax collector and was rich" (Luke 19:2). Jesus had come into Jericho and the crowds were pressing in. Zacchaeus feels some compulsion to see this teacher (fascination), but is a small man and needs to climb a sycamore tree to get a glimpse of Jesus. He is on the fringes of the crowd in more ways than one, he is an emblematic threshold figure. There are many people up trees in and around the Church, looking in, drawn to something, waiting for a sign of welcome. Jesus singles him out and invites himself to his house, much to the annoyance of the Sunday congregation: "All who saw it began to grumble and said, 'He has gone to be the guest of one who is a sinner'" (19:7). Then Zacchaeus experiences conversion and a desire to follow the ways of this man, volunteering to give away half (perhaps the other half would come later) of his possessions. In case anyone is still in any doubt Luke underlines the point that "the Son of Man came to seek out and to save the lost" (Luke 19:10).

This approach is derived from the kind of God Jesus believes in; it could not be otherwise. Jesus acts out of his understanding of God, as we all do. In Christian thinking, Jesus is the revelation of God. If Jesus consistently welcomed the outcast to the table, against the values and norms of the time, then that tells us something very fundamental about the nature of God. What the table fellowship of Jesus might mean for our understanding of the Eucharist and who we welcome (or don't) to that table was very much on the mind of the bishops when they met in Rome in October 2014 and 2015 for the synods on marriage and the family. Many in the Church believe it is time to imitate more closely the behaviour of our Lord in his unconditional welcome at table for sinners.

The revolution

In "The Joy of the Gospel", Pope Francis reminds us that the ministry of Jesus was full of encounters with people, especially the lost and the least. In fact, this is how we get to know him, in his encounters with people. The Church at different points in its history has seemed remote from ordinary people. Today the tourists meander in the grounds of the magnificent Renaissance villas on the outskirts of Rome which the cardinal princes of the Church made their home. One young seminarian at the English College in Rome in the 1960s recalled how at the beginning of Vatican II the bishops were taken from the college to the Council sessions in limousines. By the end of the Council they were travelling together in a bus.

Today we have a pope who is driven around in the back of a Ford Focus and the staff at the papal summer residence are at something of a loose end since Pope Francis chooses to stay in Rome during the hot summer months rather than cool off in the swimming pool at Castel Gandolfo. We have no difficulty, it seems, in losing sight from time to time of the radical power and point of the Gospel. With acute psychological insight, Francis exhorts those who claim to belong to Jesus to "stop looking for those personal or communal niches which shelter us from the maelstrom of human misfortune" (*EG*, 270). The Gospel path is one of compassion, reconciliation and self-emptying, which Francis sums up in the following beautiful passage:

> … the Gospel tells us constantly to run the risk of a face to face encounter with others, with their physical presence which challenges us with their pain and their pleas… True faith in the incarnate Son of God is inescapable from self-giving, from membership in the community, from service, from reconciliation with others. The Son of God, by becoming flesh, summoned us to the revolution of tenderness. (*EG*, 88)

If this is a revolution then that could be its manifesto, were it not for the fact that we already have the manifestos in the shape of the four Gospels. As we have said already, Jesus was executed in public not because he spoke platitudes or conventional wisdom. His revolution was not a call to arms either; in fact it was quite the reverse. Like any good Jew he taught that: "You shall love the Lord your God with all your heart" (Deuteronomy 6:5).

He went further and profoundly linked love of God with love of neighbour (Luke 10:27) and revealed that according to the mind of God you could not do one without the other (Matthew 25:31-46).

And just in case we settled for some comfortable position where we understood our neighbour as those we got on with in our own group, he made it clear that our neighbour included the unsightly human wreckage by the side of the road and, most radically of all, our *enemies* and those who hate us (Luke 6:27). We have succeeded in largely ignoring this, because that is what it is easier to do when faced with a summons to revolution, especially a revolution which calls for uncompromising and inclusive compassion, reconciliation and service, with no place for status, power or possessions.

Gems from the Treasure Box #6

Here is the God I want to believe in: a Father who, from the beginning of creation, has stretched out his arms in merciful blessing, never forcing himself on anyone, but always waiting, never letting his arms drop down in despair, but always hoping that his children will return so that he can speak words of love to them and let his tired arms rest on their shoulders. His only desire is to bless.

Henri Nouwen,
The Return of the Prodigal Son

The revolution calls for this because this is the nature of its source: God, the holy mystery, maker of the universe, as revealed in Jesus. And because Jesus told stories we don't have paragraphs of dry definitions telling us about God; we have images, which stay longer in the mind: like an ungainly middle-aged father who runs over the fields to welcome an errant son home before he has even heard his woeful excuses for wandering off (Luke 15:11-32).

Comments from the twelve on
Jesus and the Gospels:

I grew up in a family with revolutionary people, very much social justice, equality. I don't want to talk about politics or anything but they were very much into that. When I then met Christ the Revolutionary, the true revolutionary, that just inspired me. So when I start reading what he used to speak, when he spoke about the beatitudes, that is just the whole Gospel, so profound. Also, the way he didn't care what people thought about him, he just went ahead and listened to what God told him, what the Father told him and he just went because he lived by conviction. It's different when you live by conviction and when you live because you do things because you have to. He was moved by compassion, what an intense, strong man he was. That part of him being a man yet because of him now I am saved and no matter what I do I can still see my Father face to face, it just blew me away. His teaching is outstanding.

Emiliana, 45, charity co-founder

As Catholics we were not readers of scriptures because the only time we got involved with scriptures is when we attended Mass and then you get the Gospels read. The little things that I learned from Old Testament were in Advent when they read the prophecies, things like that. When I took the course in Biblical Studies there were a lot more interesting things and I did remember a teacher in Old Testament telling me you may not read certain parts of scriptures because they have obscenities and I was thinking: "Scriptures? Sounds interesting." So I went to the library, looked through the commentaries and looked for these. Of course you begin to discover everything else: the story of Noah, Job, Jonah, the Gospel of Luke, all of those things, and you get interested and I remember my teacher telling me, "I told you, you're not supposed to read it." "But, Father, I read them already."

Archie, 65, teacher of religion

I think I had a bit of a bug about the faith, but I did actually undergo (this is a bit embarrassing normally to talk about) a kind of conversion experience when I was fourteen, which sociologically no doubt can be analysed as a teenage whatever. But that was a big event for me because I kind of did feel the whole of the Catholic stuff didn't quite make sense and it wasn't internalised. This conversion experience actually added an inner dimension that I still know is the source of my remaining a Catholic. So I think it was pretty well from that point on I knew I wanted to either do two things; become a Jesuit and teach in universities and do social action stuff; or I wanted to be a university professor who would teach theology. I went for option B because as a university student I suddenly realised I couldn't do the celibacy.

I'm someone who likes comfort, who likes being not in pain and I don't like suffering but I am aware more and more that the levels of selfishness and self-plan in my own life are remarkably high. One doesn't become a professor or a headteacher of anything without having a lot of structure, goals, organisation, etc. There's a good thing about that and then for me I discover there's also a dark side, which is that I do control my own reality to such an extent. So for me, Jesus being saviour is just having a glimpse of what not controlling my own reality might look like and being present in an attitude of love and service in my job, towards my family, towards my extended family and friends and on a political sphere.

Greg, 56, university teacher

So reading the Bible for yourself involves bringing the horizon of what you currently think is the case to the Bible and allowing it to challenge you and change what you think. So for me it's important to keep reading the Bible, even though I've read it a lot of times before because every time you read it you see something different and it's challenging you in a different way. So I come to the Bible, if I read a story I'm finding myself quite often now reading the Bible just say, seeing a context, at the moment I'm reading readings at daily Mass and I'm finding that to study the Bible in that way, in the concentrated pattern of the themes and the season is really interesting and I'm seeing new things in it but with the *Lectio Divina* method you put yourself into the passage and say, if I was in this passage where would I be?", "What would Jesus be saying to me, am I the Pharisee or am I the person he's trying to talk to? Where am I in this story? What do I need to hear from him?"

Wendy, 52, teacher

I wouldn't say I sit down and think "I'm going to read the Gospels now" but what I didn't realise was quite how important the parables I've read had been to me. They're so simple. Parables like the Good Samaritan, which I must have read when I was five or six years old or had it read to me; they're like fables of the Bible. They've grounded my moral compass so much and helped me to understand what it actually means to be a good Christian. It's really hard, I think, for a young person to interpret the complicated nature of the scriptures and the Bible, but for me it's nice they're easy to relate to, that they're on a common, normal person's level. They're things that are very easy to happen, common occurrences. There are people who suffer and there are people that would walk past that person and there are people that would stop and for me, reading those has helped me to be the sort of person that would stop and not be the sort of person that would walk on and I think that when you're reading them when you're a child you don't necessarily think "this is how I'm going to act when I'm older" but reflecting on it now as a young adult, it's been really important to me and made the Bible much more accessible.

Xita, 20, student

It's really interesting, being a clergyman at any time from medieval, even prior to that, all the way up to the early twentieth century – Anglican, Catholic or any of these denominations – was a symbol of authority, power, social status. Now it's very much a kind of, a bit rebellious, and people like that. I've chatted with seminarians about this and there is this sort of "actually we quite like being a bit rebellious and it's our way of rebelling against society". Forty years ago maybe it would have been a hidden movement but actually in our way, and everyone thinks we're really socially conservative, but equally in our weird way we're actually choosing a different way of life, almost in a protest. There is a radical element to following Jesus and I think that's quite attractive to a lot of people and still is.

Paul, 23, chaplaincy assistant

In some ways Protestants, good Protestants are more prepared for the state of mind that can accept the real presence because they are more in love with Jesus himself, they could understand why he would want to have a kind of steady physical communication with people he loves.

Tom, 78, retired schoolmaster

Reflections for individuals

- In your journal write down your own impressions of Jesus, from childhood to the present day.

- Which of the calls of the disciples in the Gospels resonate most with you and why?

- How do you respond to the reflections of the twelve – do any of them strike a chord with you?

Reflection activity for groups

- Read the Gospel of Luke with a particular focus on the poor and table fellowship. Take two or three examples and look at them in more detail: where would you put yourself in the story, how does it challenge your own community and the way you welcome the least and the lost?

Resources for further study

The *New Revised Standard Version of the Bible* (*NRSV*) was published in 1989 and has received the widest acclaim and broadest support from academics and church leaders of any modern English translation. The translation used in the Mass is the *Jerusalem Bible* (*JB*). The *NRSV* is in the tradition of the King James Bible and is perhaps more literal than the *JB*. Different translations will suit different purposes. Raymond Brown offers useful advice on translations (see below).

Raymond E. Brown, *101 Questions on the Bible* (New York: Paulist Press, 1990). This is an excellent introduction to scripture study by the most influential Catholic scripture scholar of the twentieth century, in the opinion of many. Written in a very accessible Q&A style, many of the big questions are covered here: virgin birth, bodily resurrection, to name but two.

Universalis website (www.universalis.com). This website will provide the daily Mass readings free. Subscribers can access many other layers of prayer resources, such as the daily office of the Church. For those who wish to get to know scripture by following the daily lectionary of the Church (a rich and rewarding experience) this is highly recommended.

Notes

[1] Second Vatican Council, *Dei Verbum* [Dogmatic Constitution on Divine Revelation], 22 http://www.vatican.va/archive/hist_councils/ii_vatican_council/documents/vat-ii_const_19651118_dei-verbum_en.html, accessed 25 July 2015

[2] *Instruction on the Historical Truth of the Gospels,* http://www.catholicculture.org/culture/library/view.cfm?recnum=1352, accessed 1 November 2014

[3] Brown, *101 Questions on the Bible* (New York: Paulist Press, 1990), 56-57

[4] Denis McBride C.Ss.R., *Jesus and the Gospels* (Chawton: Redemptorist Publications, 2006), 27

[5] Brown, *101 Questions on the Bible*, 66

[6] McBride, *Jesus and the Gospels*, 28

[7] Gerard W. Hughes SJ, *God of Surprises* (London: Darton, Longman and Todd, 1996), 62

[8] *Compendium of the Catechism of the Catholic Church*, 360

[9] Raymond E. Brown, *The Gospel of Luke*, 3 Audio CD Set (Penley: Welcome Recordings, 2011)

[10] Pope Francis, *Evangelii Gaudium* [The Joy of the Gospel], 198

[11] Denis McBride C.Ss.R., *The Parables of Jesus* (Chawton: Redemptorist Publications,1999), 29

[12] McBride, *Parables of Jesus*, 71

[13] Hughes, *God of Surprises*, 69

[14] T. Keating, *Invitation to Love* (London: Bloomsbury, 2011), 11

[15] McBride, *Jesus and the Gospels*, p. 122

"Stay with us" – the death and resurrection of hope in the early disciples

It was never going to end well. From the beginning of his public ministry Jesus antagonised the religious authorities of the day. In Chapter 6 of Luke's Gospel the scribes and Pharisees are watching him to see if he would cure on the Sabbath. Jesus never seems to take the easy road. Luke tells us that he knew what they were thinking but went ahead and cured the man with the withered hand right there in front of them, on the Sabbath, and rather predictably they were "filled with fury and discussed with one another what they might do to Jesus" (Luke 6:11). It was never going to end well for Jesus or his disciples. He was adamant that the obsession of the religious authorities with legalism, exclusivity and ritualism did not fit his vision of the kingdom of God, especially the way vulnerable people should be treated.

There is in the memory of the early Church a tradition that Jesus was strongly tempted by a more worldly kingdom. In Luke's Gospel this is spelled out in some detail. Before Jesus begins his public ministry he struggles with Satan's version of the kingdom: material gain, glory and authority, empty spectacle. We might assume that the source of this tradition was Jesus himself, presumably in conversation with his disciples (how else would they know?). Whether there was an actual forty-day trial in the wilderness or the evangelists are just making use of the biblical number for exile, the point is that these temptations were *distortions of the kingdom* and Luke is careful to note that Satan left him "until an opportune time" (Luke 4:13) which would come at the Last Supper. Having failed to distort the message of the kingdom, Satan would in the end convince one of the disciples to hand over the king. We have struggled with these distortions ever since and in the Church we have given in to them at different times, falling prey to the lure of power and spectacle. If Jesus also struggled with these distortions, it was a decisive moment for him when they were cast out from his vision. When the angry men were closing in on him, one option he had ruled out was to dominate them. Before long, he was in their hands.

When he arrives in Jerusalem at the beginning of the end of his ministry, there is in each of the Gospels a scene of public disorder in the Temple (although John for his own reasons has it at the beginning). Jesus is inflamed by what he sees: buying and selling in his father's house. Luke's Gospel is the least vivid in detail, since he doesn't like portraying Jesus in anger, but he is deeply disturbed because they were "selling things" (Luke 19:45) in what should have been a place of prayer. Jesus clearly could not bear the corruption of his Father's house. He does not simply speak out against this, or resort to a parable, but he is stirred to physical action and drives out the money-changers. Luke does not say how his disciples reacted to this righteous anger but he tells us that afterwards the chief priests, scribes and leaders of the people were "looking for a way to kill him" (Luke 19:47). A prophet who criticised or attacked the Temple in Jerusalem, the source of religious authority (and income) for the religious leaders, never lasted long. Jeremiah called the Temple a "den of robbers" (Jeremiah 7:11) and ended up in a cistern, up to his neck in mud.

At the beginning of Luke's Gospel, Satan tried but failed to distort Jesus' vision of the kingdom, but he comes back at the end of Luke's Gospel and "entered into Judas" (Luke 22:3). Satan will be able to put an end to the earthly life of Jesus but that is his only victory. Before they sit down for their Passover meal Judas has made contact with the enemies of Jesus. The trap is laid. Jesus now has very little time left with his disciples. He takes a loaf of bread, gives thanks, breaks it, gives it to them and says: "This is my body, which is given for you" (Luke 22:19). He then shares his distress that one of them at the table, one who had travelled the road of discipleship, has betrayed him. In the meantime what are they arguing about? Which of them is the number one disciple! The followers of Jesus have been arguing about this ever since but Jesus, as always, puts them right: the leader must be "like the youngest" (Luke 22:26) since Jesus is among them as "one who serves" (Luke 22:27). It sounds like a simple enough point but we have consistently chosen to ignore it over the years. Those who lead in the Church are called to be servants. Nobody should be lording it over anybody else. That was always one of the great attractions in belonging to the Church in the early days.

What happens next in each of the Gospels is a study of discipleship under intense pressure: what do you do when you see the one you have followed cracking? Jesus in the garden of Gethsemane is portrayed very differently by each of the Gospel writers, according to their "version" of Jesus. The disciples are also portrayed very differently. In Mark's Gospel, the disciples fail abjectly. They fall into a "sleep of avoidance" while Jesus collapses in a state of anguish. When the arresting party arrives they scarper and one of them even leaves behind his clothes in the hands of the guards. The same people who dropped their nets to follow Jesus now drop their underwear to get away from him. It is a scene of utter humiliation.

In Luke's Gospel the disciples are treated more sympathetically, which again is perhaps why Luke is a better starting point for those on the threshold today. While Jesus prays "on his knees" (not on his face as in Mark) the disciples fall asleep "because of grief" (Luke 22:46). It is a very benign portrait of sensitive disciples. There is not even any reference to them running away in Luke's Gospel. What is recounted, of course, in all four Gospels, is the established memory of the denial of the one who was regarded as the lead disciple: Peter, the rock.

It must be of some comfort to those on the threshold of discipleship to know that following Jesus is not a straight path towards sanctification. The human path is always twisted. Sometimes we get it together, sometimes we drift. Jesus predicted that Peter would deny him when the pressure was really on, but uniquely in Luke's Gospel Jesus gives him a way back even before the denial when he says, "I have prayed for you that your own faith may not fail; and you, when once you have turned back, strengthen your brothers" (Luke 22:32). In Luke's denial scene, there is a moment of exceptional poignancy. In all the other Gospels after the arrest Jesus is taken inside for interrogation and Peter is outside.

In Luke's Gospel they are both in the courtyard of the high priest's house and when Peter denies Jesus a third time and the cock crows: "The Lord turned and looked at Peter" (Luke 22: 61). It would not seem consistent with the way Jesus is portrayed in Luke's Gospel to regard that look as one of reproach. Rather, it can be seen as a reminder of the promise to pray for him, perhaps also a reminder of the words Jesus used when Peter was called: "Do not be afraid" (Luke 5:10). It is a beautifully human moment of personal encounter when the Lord holds the weak disciple in a loving gaze.

And then the most difficult part: the Lord is executed in a wholly degrading way. Whether the disciples saw it or not, they knew what it was all about. The Romans crucified their victims in very public places as a deterrent to anyone who was thinking of getting out of line, or promoting alternative kingdoms. The victims were stripped naked, thrown to the ground and nailed by the forearms to a 100-pound cross-beam (*patibulum*) they had carried to the place of execution (although in the synoptic Gospels this is carried for the weakened Jesus by Simon of Cyrene, which suggests that the flogging was particularly harsh). They were then hoisted up attached to the *patibulum* which was slotted into the upright beam. This was probably in place permanently at the execution site, most likely on the way into the city (hence all the passers-by). It must have been a gruesome bloodstained place at the best of times. The feet were then nailed, perhaps side on to the stake. Death was caused by blood loss, asphyxiation and trauma. Some victims lasted for days but the tradition is that Jesus died quickly, perhaps because of great loss of blood. The last voices he may have heard in his final self-emptying were the taunts of those around him.

What things?

For the disciples who had travelled with Jesus and whose curiosity had deepened beyond fascination into a desire to follow this prophet, it was a bleak and bitter ending. We find two of them in Luke's Gospel walking away from Jerusalem on the first day of the week, the Sunday, two days after the death of Jesus. They are walking away from the scene of disaster, even though they have already heard about the empty tomb. It is interesting to note that an empty tomb is not enough to restore their faith. They were "astounded" (Luke 24:22) when they heard about it, but they did not equate this with resurrection. Luke is a master of dramatic irony and allows us to view the bedraggled disciples as ignorant of the fact that the stranger who joins them on the road is the risen Jesus. This makes them seem so much more vulnerable, lost and in need. They are in many ways a type, an exemplar, of the modern disciple walking away from the scene of disillusionment. They "had hoped" (Luke 24:21) for great things from their prophet, but now they are sad.

This is not an unusual scene in the Church. Throughout history and in my experience certainly in recent times there have been many disciples who have walked away from the scene of their disappointment with heavy hearts. Many Catholics have struggled with the revelations of child abuse in the Church and the way it was handled. In my Catholic youth that wasn't the problem but people struggled with darkness in other ways. A phrase that was sometimes whispered back then was that he or she (mostly he) had "lost his faith" – this was the ultimate crisis. It often referred to the more mysterious aspects of the faith, such as the Real Presence in the Eucharist.

In his CD set *Jesus and the Gospels* (See "Resources" at the end of the chapter) Denis McBride tells the sad story of a priest who lost his faith and whose only prayer was that of Mary Magdalene: "They have taken away my Lord and I don't know where they have laid him" (John 20:13). The priest in question stayed in the priesthood, doing what good he could, since as he wryly observed who would want to employ an old atheist in a cassock! The story of Emmaus has relevance for every age.

The irony deepens when they tell him that he must be the only one who hasn't heard about the things that had happened in Jerusalem, not knowing that the stranger was at the excruciating centre of the drama. In another moment of great poignancy Jesus asks the deflated disciples to share their pain with him by asking the shortest question in the New Testament: "What things?" (24:19) – *tell me what's in your heart.* Jesus then instructs them in the scriptures and they realise that their discipleship is not dead, only dormant. When he makes as if to go on they know they do not want to be parted from this stranger who somehow has been able to touch their sorry hearts: "Stay with us, because it is almost evening and the day is now nearly over" (24:29). He does stay and at the breaking of the bread they finally recognise him, only for him to vanish. But Luke is reminding his own community they have had the sustenance which is available to Christians of all ages: the scripture and the Eucharist. They are on fire now and run back to Jerusalem, *to the community*, where they find a group of disciples in a state of confused excitement – "The Lord has risen indeed, and he has appeared to Simon!" (Luke 24:34). On the other side of crucifixion another look is exchanged, but this one is beyond words.

Last of all he appeared to me

The modern mind struggles with the resurrection of Jesus, and many disciples on the way into or out of the Church question the historicity of this event. Because the resurrection stories are all so different some scholars have indeed cast doubt on the historical veracity of the resurrection. The modern mind can easily convince itself that what we are hearing is the witness of a community that came to realise that the spirit of Jesus was alive in their hearts and his message lived on through them. Despite my doubts, that has never satisfied me and I have found very helpful advice from one of our trusted guides, Raymond E. Brown. He explains his understanding of the resurrection this way:

> I maintain that the biblical evidence points to the fact that Peter and Paul preached a risen Jesus whose body had not corrupted in the grave. There is not an iota of New Testament evidence that any Christian thought the body of Jesus was still in the grave corrupting. Therefore, I think that the biblical evidence greatly favours the corporeal resurrection of Jesus.[1]

There are many other corroborating arguments for the resurrection. Brown reminds us that despite the differences in the details of the accounts there is a solid tradition in each of the four Gospels that the tomb was empty on Easter morning. It is also worthy of note that the main witness to this in the Gospels is Mary Magdalene. If the early Christians wanted a reliable and authoritative witness as defined by the contemporary culture, they would have opted for a respectable male, like Joseph of Arimathea. The legal status of women in first-century Palestine, where they could not testify in legal proceedings, is a very compelling argument that Mary was in fact the core witness. They were telling the truth, because they could have done so much better with their prime witness had they been canny. There is also of course the circumstantial point that no non-believer ever came forward at any point to contradict Christian claims of resurrection by pointing to a body in a tomb.

Then there is Paul. He was not an eyewitness to the life and death of Jesus but scholars seem to agree that he was converted within two to three years of the crucifixion. He calls himself an apostle since, like the other apostles, he has seen the risen Christ. Writing to his community of converts in Corinth only twenty or so years after his own conversion, Paul summarises the established tradition of post-resurrection appearances. The risen Christ first appeared to Cephas (Peter), then the twelve, then to more than five hundred brothers and sisters, then to James, the brother of Jesus and "last of all, as to someone untimely born, he appeared also to me" (1 Corinthians 15:8). Paul is adamant that without the resurrection the faith he preaches would be pointless: "If Christ has not been raised, your faith is futile" (15:17). Brown reminds us that the nature of the resurrected body of Christ is quite different from the Jesus who walked among the disciples on earth. The Gospels make this clear when they talk of the risen Christ not being recognised and able to appear suddenly and disappear. Brown comments:

> There is no doubt that Paul maintains that what was sown in the grave is raised with very different properties. There is an enormous transformation of the body… Paul thinks of bodily resurrection, but the transformation indicated by his words seems to take the risen body out of the realm of the physical into the spiritual. [2]

And what does the risen Christ in the Gospels tell us about God, more than Jesus told us? You would expect the messages to be consistent. Disciples might be confused if we went from a compassionate, healing, inclusive historical Jesus to a triumphalist, legalistic, threatening risen Christ.

75

But that is not what we find. The few words attributed to the risen Christ seem at one with the nature of the historical Jesus. In Luke's Gospel the first words of the risen Christ are: "Peace be with you" (Luke 24:36). There is no mention of the events of the passion, who let him down or the settling of scores. There is no display of power in the earthly sense. This has already been ruled out as a distortion of the kingdom by Luke in the early chapters of his Gospel. There is only peace and reconciliation. The disciples of course are still terrified and he reassures them that it is the same Lord, but different. Like on the road to Emmaus, he opens their minds to understand the scriptures and he provides them with a succinct summary of what they have to proclaim to the nations: "repentance and forgiveness of sins" (Luke 24:47). That is not so different from the physical Jesus who strode through the pages of Luke dining with the wrong people, healing and forgiving with no precondition and saying change your mind, your way of looking at the world.

Lord and saviour

In terms of theology, what does the resurrection mean? I can only speak as an ordinary disciple but from my readings and reflections the resurrection seems to suggest that God has transformed the brutal realities of existence into glory. If the punctured dead body of the wonder-worker hanging outside the city walls of Jerusalem had been the end, then there would be no hope from that quarter; we would be left to our own resources. The disciples on the road would have kept walking and settled into lives of quietly permanent disappointment. We would struggle along to find our own meaning and defences against brutality, lining up our pleasures, our art, our helpful clever formulations, but death in the end would loom over us in terrible finality. There are many brave and good people (and just many people) who live their lives like that, with no belief in a greater reality, in life after death, in God. For me it has always been a deep motivation to hang on in the Church, since the prospect of living without the meaning the Church provides is unbearable. That is perhaps a kind of existential cowardice, but I just don't have the stomach for nihilism (*nihil*, as in the Latin "nothing").

In the crucifixion God in Jesus absorbed the full brutality of the human condition unto death and did not resist, retaliate or throw it back as we normally do. The usual pattern was interrupted and transformed. A cycle of endless vicious retaliation (eye for an eye) on an individual, tribal and national level was stopped at that point. In Luke's Gospel Jesus utters forgiveness from the cross. I cannot imagine that those words were spoken just for the little agitated cohort of humanity in front of him: Jesus was forgiving our faults, the human condition, *forgiving fallen reality*. He reconciled us to God. Pope Francis says that: "Jesus endured in his own flesh the dramatic encounter of the sin of the world and God's mercy…"[3]

Gems from the Treasure Box #7

As the inner life of the prisoner tended to become more intense, he also experienced the beauty of art and nature as never before. Under their influence he sometimes even forgot his own frightful circumstances. If someone had seen our faces on the journey from Auschwitz to a Bavarian camp as we beheld the mountains of Salzburg with their summits glowing in the sunset, through the little barred windows of the prison carriage, he would never have believed that those were the faces of men and women who had given up all hope of life and liberty. Despite that factor – or maybe because of it – we were carried away by nature's beauty, which we had missed for so long.

Viktor E. Frankl,
Man's Search for Meaning

The sin of the world (original sin) is what we are born into. In truth, we do not know what we are doing but Jesus forgives that and points the way to living according to the mind of God. The wonder of Easter morning was that the broken body of God was transformed so that suffering from now on could be seen as not entirely futile but in the end taken up and transformed in glory. Love is the last word. The revolution of tenderness has begun. Gerard W. Hughes puts it this way, in a memorable passage from *God of Surprises*:

> In Christ, who is God, human sin and God's goodness meet in the same person. Christ absorbs the pain in himself and prays: "Father forgive them." When human sin had done its worst, God in Christ, replies with the blood and water from his pierced side. God's love is greater than human hatred and has won a victory for ever. This is the triumph and the joy of the cross. Evil has been confronted, has been allowed to do its worst to God in the humanity of Christ, and God in Christ transforms this evil act into victory through love.[4]

In my conversations with the twelve and in my own experience with fellow pilgrims in the Church, it is clear that most of us struggle with the meaning of Jesus as our personal Lord and saviour. We were brought up with a story of human history that told us how two individuals in primeval times disobeyed God and that caused us to fall from grace (see Paul's comments). This sin had to be atoned for to restore our relationship with God and, to do that, God sent his only Son to die horribly at the hands of men. But a God who demands innocent blood is not consistent with the father of the prodigal son, the obsessive hunter after the lost sheep, the lost coin.

Science also tells us that our progenitors evolved over many millions of years and to pick out one or two who disobeyed is clearly not historical but is an attempt to explain why human nature has been such a beautifully flawed and fallen experience *from the beginning.*

The Church has different traditions of understanding the saving mission of Jesus other than a narrative of atonement which changed God's mind about us (see "Resources": *Christianity in Evolution).* Richard Rohr, the American Franciscan, comments that: "Jesus is not changing his Father's mind about us; he is changing our mind about what is real and what is not."[5] That makes more sense to me. For too long we worshipped and admired the sacrifice of Jesus, thinking all the work had been done for us, our sins had been washed away. We thought that to follow him had something to do with matching that level of suffering as repentance.

In the film *Calvary* (2014), a priest is told in confession that he will be killed in one week's time to make up for the sexual abuse suffered in childhood by the stranger on the other side of the grille. The priest who committed the abuse is dead, but the priest who will be killed is a good man. It sounds as if he will be the innocent sacrifice to atone for the sins of the abuser, but that is the pained logic of the victim and not the logic of God. In the week that follows the confessional threat, the Church in Ireland is shown to be on its own road to Calvary after the devastating revelations of child abuse, especially in the report of Justice Seán Ryan (2009). The priest is routinely ridiculed and at one point a father delivers a volley of abuse to him for talking to his daughter who had wandered off by herself.

When I entered senior seminary in Ireland in 1980 few people knew then that it was the last days of an era. The Church at the time was strong, confident, respected. Some would say authoritarian, arrogant and complacent. My seminary was one of twelve in the country, each with around 150 young men in training for holy orders. It was, looking back, something of a production line. A cynic would say that the priesthood was not a bad career option for the third son. It was a degree-level education followed by a comfortable middle-class existence and a respectable role in the community. The churches were busy on a Sunday, the pope had visited the previous year, the Catholic clubs and sodalities were in full swing. It was the last days of the Catholic culture. What came next was a kind of crucifixion, a dramatic collapse in faith in the Church due largely to the shocking revelations of the crimes of its trusted members. In 1984 there were 171 ordinations to the priesthood in Ireland, in 2006 there were twenty-two and in 2015, fourteen. Today there is one senior seminary in Ireland.

Calvary is of course a fictional dramatisation of that story but from the accounts of those who have lived through the trauma it does capture well the seismic shift that had taken place. In the week before the priest is shot by the victim of abuse, we see him minister to the people of his community as well as he can with humour and patience. He does go back on the drink but that seems understandable after the church is set on fire and his beloved dog is killed. In the final reckoning on the beach he is shot dead, but that is not the final scene. His daughter (his wife died and then he became a priest) visits the man who killed her father in prison. We have already witnessed a scene of reconciliation when she forgives her father for abandoning her and he forgives her for attempting to take her own life. The final scene captures the face of the murderer/victim on the verge of being forgiven, which is a resurrection for them both.

Gems from the Treasure Box #8

Our awakening to the presence and action of the Spirit is the unfolding of Christ's resurrection in us.

Thomas Keating,
Open Mind, Open Heart

Christ is risen

In many periods of the Church's history it seemed as if the resurrection had been forgotten, and the morbid focus was on the suffering and death of the Lord. It is of course the darkest moment in human history. We had the revelation of God with us in the person of Jesus for a few short years and we flogged him and killed him. Before this shameful scene the Church falls to its knees, as it should. But sometimes we have forgotten to get back up off our knees because that is not the end of the story. In the Catholic culture described in Chapter 1 we did Lent very well, from the ashes thumbed onto our foreheads which reminded us that we were dust and would one day be dust again, to the purple-shrouded mourning of Good Friday afternoon. Pope Francis reminds us, with characteristic straight talking, that "there are some Christians whose lives seem like Lent without Easter" (*EG*, 6). And this is not a summons to a glib and superficial happiness. This pope has known and seen suffering. The summons for all Christians is that, despite the real suffering faced by many, "slowly but surely we all have to let the joy of faith revive as a quiet yet firm trust, even amid the greatest distress" (*EG*, 6).

Christ *is* risen, as we often say at Mass. This is the foundation for our joy and our hope. In the next chapter we will consider the ways in which we understand the presence of Jesus Christ to be still with us. It is also worth reflecting on resurrection not just as something which happened to Jesus, but, as Richard Rohr describes it in *Immortal Diamond*, a universal pattern or journey which is the way of all things and the way to God. Some kind of dying is necessary before we are transformed and become "like him" (1 John 3:2). For much of Christian history we assumed that it was the body, or the pleasures of the body, which had to "die" and we set about mortifying the body, sometimes in extreme fashion. Perhaps I am just a soft child of the modern age, but that is not how I understand the journey of Christian discipleship. What has to die, as Rohr says, inspired by Thomas Merton and the revival of the contemplative tradition in the last century, is what he calls the False Self, the ego, all that is self-obsessed within us. We will look at that in more detail in Chapter 6.

We are called to be more like Jesus Christ and to grow in grace, the life of God. I believe that this is what holiness means. Vatican II brought grace back into the realm of the ordinary (see: Gems #2, #12). Grace was not some divine juice that was turned on and off depending on how good we had been that week. Grace is the ever present invitation to participate in the life of God which is "not far from each one of us" (Acts 17:27). Grace is what transforms us and every step towards that transformation it like a resurrection. We used to believe that it was all about getting to heaven, but the modern prophets are more inclined to say that it is about experiencing heaven now: in every word or gesture of love, of reaching out, of taking the first step even though it hurts your pride. If somehow grace has allowed you to transform your default reaction, that is a resurrection: the little resurrections of the heart.

Rohr invites us to consider a very human reaction to resurrection in Mark's Gospel. The original version of the Gospel finishes at 16:8: "So they went and fled from the tomb, for terror and amazement had seized them; and they said nothing to anyone, for they were afraid." As the oldest Gospel there is an assumption that this might be the most historically accurate. It probably took the disciples quite a while to come to terms with resurrection. Their first reaction was to run, which Rohr interprets as "the human temptation to run from and deny not just the divine presence, but our own true selves, that is our souls, our inner destiny, our true identity". 6 Jesus was trying to school his disciples in a new form of his presence, beyond the physical, and a new form of life, beyond the cross. James' comments at the end of this chapter offer a remarkable insight into the resurrection. We often regard the cross as the great scandal of history, the death of our Lord. James argues that the real scandal, the real challenge for us, is to live in the reality of the resurrection which summons us to be transformed and to live in a transformed reality. We will look in more detail in later chapters at what that transformation might look like for disciples.

The disciples were distraught when their Lord, who had won their hearts and whom they believed in, was led

Gems from the Treasure Box #9

The love of God passes by radiantly, the Holy Spirit goes through every person in his night like a lightning bolt. In this passing the risen Lord lays hold of you, he burdens himself with everything that is unbearable and takes it all upon himself. Only afterward, often much, much later, do you realize: Christ passed by and bestowed grace out of his superabundance.

Brother Roger Schütz, quoted in *The Youth Catechism of the Catholic Church*

away like a criminal and executed. They were then elated, some sooner than others, when they came to understand that he had been raised from the dead into glory. The journey would go on, the conversation would continue in a different way. They were not alone, their Lord was with them on the road. Their Lord was with them in his word and in the breaking of the bread. The Lord was also with them in their community, and how that community came to be formed we will now consider.

Comments from the twelve on the death and resurrection of Jesus

I think saviour of the world is quite a difficult phrase to relate to as a layperson might not necessarily be completely immersed in all the teachings of the Church. I definitely see Jesus Christ as a saviour of the world but I see it through him being a teacher. He came to help; his sacrifice was to save humanity from sin, and understanding that is the key point. It almost validates all those things that he then goes on to teach about how you should be a good person. Knowing that ultimate sacrifice he made and that God made helps you to think his teachings are so important and so valuable. Indeed, they were so important to him he gave his life, and that really helps me to understand him as the saviour of the world and want to follow his teachings.

It makes me feel like if I follow his teachings the things that I perhaps do that are wrong can be forgiven because that's why he gave his life and died on the cross for us. He's definitely a teacher figure to me and I think when you're young it's a lot easier to understand something in relation to what you know. I'm still being taught every day, I'm at university, I've got my lecturers, I can understand the relationship between a student and a teacher and that's how my relationship with Jesus has been. I'm the student, he's the teacher and because of that I can really appreciate and value that idea that he is the saviour of the world.

Xita, 20, student

I don't want to say anything that is heretical but certainly my understanding of sin and salvation is that it doesn't mean Adam and Eve with apples, but we seem to have been either created or there seems to be an element to us that's bad, we seem to all have that bad side to us so we are born into original sin and that's me reading people who are talking about Saint Augustine.

So there had to be a saviour for mankind. God loved the world, he gave his only Son and so Jesus gave his life willingly on the cross and obviously his blood which poured down from the cross saves humanity, my sins are paid for on that cross, I am saved, I don't mean that in the kind of, what some Evangelicals say, which means because I accept that and believe in that I'm definitely going to heaven but I'm saved in the sense my salvation's open to me but I've got to try and work at it. Not in the sense if I go to lots of Masses and therefore it's a competition of who can go to the most Masses, but by going to Mass and receiving the sacraments I'm getting closer to God and trying to grow closer in my faith.

If you said Jesus is my personal Lord and saviour, I've never got up and said that in a church, but that is true for all of us, it's just we don't get up there and say it which is what Evangelicals will do. I think as Catholics, when we're asked, it doesn't happen as much in England or the UK, in America maybe more, but if you were asked do you accept Jesus is your personal Lord and saviour, you'd say "yes I do". "Have you been born again?", "Yes I have, I've been baptised", it's just we don't use those terms but I think it's really important we know what they're saying so that when they ask us we can then say "Yes, we have".

Paul, 23, chaplaincy assistant

I've never assumed that the people I'm teaching, if I'm teaching theology, people with no formal theological background, don't know theology. What I've always assumed is that they actually do know and what I'm hoping is that what I'm talking about they will recognise because it's already given them, they're already living it. I think if you take that phrase "saviour of the world" they won't recognise it, that's a formal phrase that we use, theology uses, but if you said: "What's been the experience of Christ healing in your life or in your experience?" I bet you they'd have something to say.

In the resurrection narratives, the big struggle is to recognise his presence. Also, Christ helps us to recognise. When he calls Mary Magdalene by name then she recognises him, her eyes are opened. When he encounters his disciples and greets him, then they recognise. So Christ is always working to help us recognise his presence here amongst us. What it requires of us is a willingness, it requires a metanoia, it requires a change, a transformation. It requires us to accept that he's risen and not to start putting down conditions like: "You can't be resurrected because it's against this, it must conform to the laws of physics, or our understanding of this, that and the other."

In actual fact our world is already open to that because we know that our intellect cannot do justice to the realities of the created order, let alone the resurrected Christ. So what the resurrection calls for from us is this wonderful simply "yes" to Christ's presence, that God has done this. And you notice that the way in which the resurrection is not something we can work our way to, you can't think it, it's something that's given and we have to be open to that. So I think that it's starting there with that openness to the fact that God has done this, Christ is alive.

The great scandal is not ultimately the scandal of the cross, the world lives with that daily, it lives with the profound tragedy and the brutality of suffering, and particularly innocent suffering. We just see it all around in the wars but we also see it in these poor people who have just been trafficked in boats from Africa and all the rest of it. We see that, we live with that every day. That's terrible but in a way it's secure because that's the world that we know, that's the world that doesn't demand very much of us other than perseverance and the struggle for justice. The real scandal is in resurrection because the resurrection requires us to live in a world that is God's world, in which evil is transitory and contingent, not necessary, not built in to the order, and that's profoundly challenging because the resurrection's the basic insecurity.

James, 64, religious order

Reflections for individuals

- Contemplate if you can the image of the broken Jesus on the cross – what image of God is being presented to us?

- In your journal write down your own experience of disappointment, your lost dreams and hopes. Can you recall any moments of "resurrection" in your life, when you experienced a surge towards a more forgiving and transformed outlook on life and those around you?

- Read through the comments from the twelve and the gems from the treasure box – choose one, perhaps, that speaks to you and reflect on its message.

Reflection activity for groups

- Is your group prepared to have an honest conversation about when they have lost hope and seemed to be going in opposite directions away from the scene of disaster?

- Is your group prepared to discuss where the seeds of resurrection can be found to reinvigorate the community?

Resources for further study and reflection

Jack Mahoney SJ, *Christianity in Evolution*. In 1988, Pope John Paul II sought to open up a dialogue between evolution and religion based on a modern understanding of the science. This book is an honest and responsible response to that invitation. The author provides us with a very well-informed exploration of the theological implications of human evolution on our traditional understanding of the sacrifice of Jesus.

Denis McBride, *Jesus and the Gospels* (Chawton: Redemptorist Publications, set of 36 audio CDs). I cannot recommend this set of CDs highly enough for those who need an engaging and intelligent introduction to the Gospels, delivered with an elegant humour and helpful references to a wide range of contemporary culture. For me it was ideal listening in the car on the daily commute to work.

Timothy Radcliffe OP, *Seven Last Words* (London: Bloomsbury, 2004). In this beautiful little book, Timothy Radcliffe takes each of the traditional seven last sentences uttered by Jesus on the cross and develops meditations on suffering using examples from own times, ranging from the hostage Brian Keenan to his own experience of the genocide in Rwanda. He also develops a Christian response to three of the most challenging events in history which Christians should meditate on with great humility: the conquest of the Americas, the holocaust and 9/11.

Notes

[1] Raymond E. Brown, *101 Questions on the Bible* (New Jersey: Paulist Press, 1990), 72

[2] Brown, *101 Questions on the Bible*, 75

[3] Pope Francis, *Evangelii Gaudium* [The Joy of the Gospel], 285

[4] G.W. Hughes SJ, *God of Surprises* (London: Darton, Longman and Todd, 1985), 129

[5] Richard Rohr, *Things Hidden: Scripture as Spirituality* (Cincinnati: St Anthony Messenger Press, 2007), 189

[6] Richard Rohr, *Immortal Diamond* (London: SPCK, 2013), vii

I believe – from fascination to declaration

Some were called, and some were not. Jesus had many encounters with people but he did not always invite them to follow him: "Your faith has saved you; go in peace" (Luke 7:50). As Raymond E. Brown comments: "During Jesus' lifetime people were able to listen to him, be impressed by him, but go away without any visible sign that they had come to believe his proclamation of the kingdom."[1] There was no attempt by Jesus to organise a community (apart from the symbolic appointment of the twelve apostles but that structure did not survive their deaths), or to establish membership. The scholarly view of this seems to be that Jesus did not have to do this because he was operating within Judaism and his mission was to the lost sheep of the house of Israel. In his own mind he wasn't founding a new religion, he was reforming his own. Jesus was baptised by John but he did not baptise those who followed him.

The risen Jesus in Matthew, and in a later addition in Mark, calls for baptism but that was not a feature of his public ministry. In other words, it looks more like a **Stage 3** decision for the benefit of the evangelists' communities rather than the recollection of a **Stage 1** event. It is quite remarkable, therefore, that from the beginning of the Church that is exactly what the first preachers did. In the Acts of the Apostles, which is Luke's sequel to his Gospel, the first preaching of Peter after the resurrection (Acts 2:38) calls for repentance (*metanoia*), which is what Jesus called for, *and* he calls for something Jesus never insisted on in his lifetime or after his resurrection in Luke's Gospel: baptism. Brown comments that "the additional demand for baptism has an interesting effect: the following of Jesus now comes to include a visible step. The demand for the visible sign by the preachers… is in a sense the first step towards organising the believers into a visible community."[2]

This is not a comment on the Church's teaching on baptism, but as a sociological point it says something interesting, about not just the early Church but the Church today. From the very beginning there has been a consistent emphasis on belonging to a community that believes and proclaims Jesus as Lord. There may be some who point to the Gospels and say that Jesus didn't seem overly concerned about membership, which is true. However, the Holy Spirit's guidance of the Church tells us that belief in Jesus outside a supportive community which has authoritative teaching at its heart is almost certainly condemned from the outset to subjectivism. One of the biggest temptations for the modern disciple, who may have a general distrust of institutions (and who can blame them, given what has happened in the Church, in politics, in the press…) is to opt for a "me and Jesus" approach, or perhaps me and Jesus and a few friends. There are very many such small groups but there is a risk that at some point ego will get in the way and the group will subdivide.

There is a great attraction in joining an institution that has been struggling with the mystery of God in Jesus for two thousand years. Of course it's not perfect – that's a given with any human organisation – but it does at least provide a home, a place to return to and a sense of accountability. The adult disciple on the threshold of the Catholic Church at some point has to deal with the question of signing up. If this attraction to Jesus deepens into a claim on how I want to live my life then the Christian tradition says it needs to be followed by a public declaration: *I believe that Jesus Christ is Lord.* Evangelical Christians seem to me much more open and public about that declaration; they see it as part of their new or "born again" identity. I don't think Catholics in a totally Catholic culture, especially those baptised as infants, ever felt the need to be so public about their declaration. If in later life their cradle Catholicism deepens into intentional Catholicism then there aren't the same encouragement or opportunities to declare that they are born again – especially if they have been confirmed.

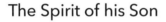

The Spirit of his Son

From the beginning they signed up in serious numbers. Luke seems to be fascinated by the numbers joining the Church in the early days: three thousand one day, six thousand the next. This can lead to a dangerous mindset when you equate growing numbers with success and you might not be able to deal so well with the time when numbers start to decline, as they are currently in the West. But in those early decades and centuries the growth of Christianity was quite astonishing. Again in sociological terms it is worth looking a little more closely at how Christianity managed to maintain its coherence for so long. There were tensions and arguments from day one, but no major schisms in the Church for almost a thousand years. How did they manage, as we might say today, *to stay on message?* In an age when communication was slow – when much of the theology, including the nature and identity of Jesus Christ was being developed – how, in the name of God, did it all hold together?

Let's go back to Paul for a moment. He describes himself in his letter to the community of Galatians written in the early AD 50s, well before any of the Gospels, as a violent persecutor of the early Church in the two to three years following the death of Jesus. Then God revealed his Son to him and his life changed, which scholars believe was around AD 35. Paul wasn't converted to Christianity, since that did not exist in AD 35 as we know it today. He was converted to *Christ*. He saw the risen Lord. He did not hear the Gospel from any human source, either, but as he tells his community in Galatia: "I received it through a revelation of Jesus Christ" (Galatians 1:12). He is so confident of his revelation that he does not confer with anyone but takes himself off on a mission to Arabia and Damascus for three years. After that, he pays a very short visit to Peter in Jerusalem. Scholars point out that the word he uses in Galatians to describe this visit (*istoresai*) suggests research, or getting acquainted, more than a social call.

It is a fascinating prospect. Within five years of the death of Jesus we have Paul back in Jerusalem. The disciples are understandably nervous about his return. He was the one who held the coats of the execution party who stoned Stephen, the first Christian martyr, to death (Acts 22:20). He was the one who led the persecution in Jerusalem: "entering house after house, dragging off both men and women, he committed them to prison" (Acts 8:3). It was probably better for all concerned five years on that he limited his contacts to Peter and James, the brother of the Lord. It is not improbable to imagine them in such a small city revisiting the scenes of the passion, perhaps praying in the garden of Gethsemane, or at Golgotha on the way into the city, with the upright stakes for crucifixion most probably still in place. This could also have been his first eyewitness contact with the life of Jesus, hearing from Peter himself the story of the public ministry, death and resurrection. The point of their intense unrecorded conversations seems to have been to make sure they were preaching one Gospel, that their essential *kerygma* (proclamation) was the same.

The next time Paul returns to Jerusalem, some fourteen years later, it is to make sure that he "was not running, or had not run, in vain" (Galatians 2:2). At the beginning of his letter Paul refers to those who "want to pervert the gospel of Christ" (Galatians 1:7). Paul is back in Jerusalem around AD 50 to try and sort out what could be a major problem: do Gentiles who wish to become Christians need to be circumcised according to the Law of Moses? Up to that point most converts to early Christianity were probably Jewish but in Paul's mission in Antioch he was converting Gentiles. The Council of Jerusalem heard evidence from the main players: Paul, Peter and James, the brother of the Lord; the one Catholics are a bit nervous about. In fact it is not Peter but *James* who makes the final authoritative pronouncement. He is clearly the leader of the Church in Jerusalem since he was of the "royal" line from Jesus. His decision, based on a close reading of scripture, is that they should "not trouble those Gentiles who are turning to God" (Acts 15:19). It is an early example of the centre holding and the efforts the key figures made to ensure a consistent Gospel, otherwise there would have been fracture from the beginning. The second millennium of Christianity has sadly not been as coherent as the first but it held together for so long, and in large part still holds, because as Paul says in his first letter to the Corinthians: "Whether then it was I or they, so we proclaim and so you have come to believe" (1 Corinthians 15:11).

For me this is one of the great appeals of being a Christian in the Catholic Church. I may struggle with some aspects of the teaching (although I believe in the doctrinal core) but I need to belong to a Christian Church which teaches with wisdom and authority. Sometimes the Church teaches with too much authority for some and goes through phases of emphasising teachings which seem quite remote from the *kerygma* of the Gospel, but it always seems to come back – or someone in the Church will always bring you back – to the radiant heart of the message found in the Gospels. Cardinal Walter Kasper reminds us that Pope Francis "recollects anew the teaching of the Second Vatican Council concerning the hierarchy of truths. It requires that the Church's many and diverse truths be interpreted from their Christological foundation (*Unitatis Redintegratio* 11; *Evangelii Gaudium* 36)".[3]

The historical Jesus is no longer with us, but in the Acts of the Apostles the Holy Spirit ("The Spirit of his Son" [Galatians 4:6]) becomes the main source of inspiration and guidance for the disciples, the guarantee of God's faithfulness. In Luke's Gospel the risen Jesus does not send the disciples out right away. In fact his instruction is to "stay here in the city" (Luke 24:49). Don't do anything. Why not? They need to be "clothed with power from on high" (24:49). They need the Holy Spirit, the active presence of God in the Church then and today.

The Holy Ghost, as he used to be called, was always a strange entity for Catholics. He was often represented as a sacred dove and I think many struggled quietly to see any link between that and their faith. When I was eight I was confirmed and I received the Holy Ghost, without really knowing much about what was supposed to be happening. After the Vatican Council there was a resurgence of the charismatic movement in the Church, when people sought to rediscover the Spirit as it was experienced in the early Church (see Emiliana's comments). The charismatics do what Catholics aren't very good at: they pray spontaneously and lift their arms from their side, led by the Spirit. They live their faith "in the Spirit" as the early Christians did, as Paul did. I believe that another of the fruits of the Council was to bring us back to the Holy Spirit, the "forgotten guest" of the pre-Vatican II Church. Fr Cantalamessa, a Franciscan Capuchin priest and Preacher to the Papal Household since 1980, provides us with the following definition of the third person of the Trinity:

> He is the only "unmediated mediation" between us and Christ in the sense that he does not act as a veil or constitute a barrier. He is not an intermediary since he is the Spirit of Jesus himself, his "alter ego", who is of the same nature. St Irenaeus reaches the point of saying that "communion with Christ... is the Holy Spirit."[4]

The Holy Spirit is the Spirit of Jesus still with us and working in us. The impact of the Spirit in the early Church is described vividly in the story of Pentecost. The role of the Spirit in the life of the early Church was not just to empower and enthuse but also to guide. Jesus did not leave us with all the answers during his lifetime. He did not have much to say about global warming or weapons of mass destruction, since they weren't issues for his society. But as we have already seen he didn't seem to have said much about the rules on becoming a Christian, which was why at the Council of Jerusalem nobody quotes Jesus. The Church has always been a community of memory, passing on what it remembers from one generation to the next. It is also a community of the Spirit, since it needs guidance from one generation to the next on the best way to deal with its current questions.

In the early preaching of Peter referred to before, after repentance and baptism comes the gift of the Holy Spirit. We should not, however, become overly schematic about this, or think for a moment that we've got the ways of God worked out. In Acts there is a wonderful example of the Holy Spirit telling us that he does not always follow our schedule. When Peter was addressing the house of Cornelius, a God-fearing Gentile, "the Holy Spirit fell upon all who heard the word" (Acts 10:44). Peter concludes that he can't withhold the water of baptism since the Spirit got there first. It is a useful reminder that in all our struggles with faith we are dealing with the holy mystery of God. We trust that this God is compassionate and loving, as revealed in the person of Jesus, but we must ultimately bring a great deal of humility to our understanding of the ways of God.

All who believed were together

Having heard the proclamation and been baptised, the first Christian communities were established. Luke provides us with one of the first descriptions of what characterised their life together: "They devoted themselves to the apostles' teaching and fellowship, to the breaking of bread and the prayers" (Acts 2:42). This is not an official or dogmatic description of a Christian community but it has a special place in the memory of the Church since it is one of the earliest. It is, therefore, a good place to start to show those on the threshold looking in what they might expect from this community, and to remind those in the Church what the community should look like, in its original form.

There is some evidence from the texts of the New Testament of what the apostles concentrated on in their teaching. It intrigues many people who come to Christianity for the first time that the apostles seem to say very little about the kingdom preaching of Jesus and all the parables which we looked at in Chapter 2. Paul makes very little reference to the public ministry of Jesus (although he was writing letters about specific issues in a community, not catechesis). The first problem the apostles had was that Jesus had been crucified after a legal process as a heretic and a criminal. It was a wretched, humiliating and very public death. This was a scandal, literally a stumbling block. Paul confronts this problem head-on, writing to the Corinthians around AD 56: "We proclaim Christ crucified, a stumbling-block to Jews and foolishness to Gentiles" (1 Corinthians 1:23).

In his first sermon, Peter sums it up as follows: "Jesus of Nazareth, a man attested to you by God with deeds of power... this man... you crucified and killed... But God raised him up, having freed him from death... Therefore let the entire house of Israel know with certainty that God has made him both Lord and Messiah, this Jesus whom you crucified" (Acts 2:22-24, 36). Nobody would pay much attention to the parables of a dead prophet whose power deserted him on a cross. Happy memories, memorable stories, but in the end the system crushed him, as the system always does. But this time it's different, this Jesus whom "you crucified" has been raised in glory and is Lord. Peter's listeners are "cut to the heart" (2:37). Luke is pleased to report that about three thousand changed their outlook that day and were baptised.

The *kerygma* involved more than just proclaiming that Jesus who had been killed has been raised by the Father and is now Lord. There are only so many times you could say that, although it is the first point that needs to be made, since it deals with the stumbling block. The rest can follow, although it's not spelled out in too much detail in Acts or in Paul's letters. Luke does say that Peter "testified with many other arguments" (Acts 2:40) and we hear later on that Paul in Ephesus "for three months spoke out boldly and argued persuasively about the kingdom of God" (19:8). The assumption is that in this *extended kerygma* the passion narrative, miracle stories, sayings and parables of Jesus were being shaped into teaching that would in time form the Gospels. As the communities developed, as the *children* of the converts came to faith, more detailed and specific ethical teaching was required, as well as some description of the norms and routines the community should follow.

There is an important distinction to be made between the *kerygma* we have been describing – the proclamation, the core message about Jesus Christ – and the more systematic teaching (*didache*) which follows. Fr Ranieri Cantalamessa puts it this way:

> Now the *didache* is the teaching, the catechesis. The important thing to know is that for the apostles and the primitive Church, faith blossoms only in front of the *kerygma*, not in front of the *didache*, the moral teaching and so on. This comes later, to form, to build, to mould the faith which has already been started. And as we are living in a situation very much similar to them, we must rediscover the *kerygma*, this fundamental message about Jesus which has the power of cutting the hearts of people.[5]

Faith blossoms in front of the *kerygma*. I believe that is why there is much emphasis on this today. In the totally Catholic culture described in Chapter 1 the *kerygma* in many ways was lost, or muffled in a cacophony of rules and regulations. Jesus himself was "lost" in the trappings of ritual. For those who have been brought up in the Church, it is possible to become lost in the labyrinth of the teaching and forget the freshness and power of the source. As we embark in the West on a phase of intentional discipleship, the *kerygma*, the proclamation, has to be heard again for those on the threshold to have any chance of coming in, or staying in. Sherry Weddell puts it this way:

> One of the obstacles to calling our own to discipleship is that few Catholics have ever heard of the *kerygma* or the "Great Story of Jesus" (to borrow a wonderful phrase from Father Robert Barron), and even fewer know what the *kerygma* contains or have heard it preached clearly.[6]

The *kerygma*, the great story of Jesus, or the core of the Christian message, is very much a central theme of "The Joy of the Gospel". Pope Francis insists that "the first proclamation must ring out over and over: Jesus Christ loves you; he gives his life to save you; and now he is living at your side every day to enlighten, strengthen and free you".[7] He is taking us back to our very beginnings but not in a nostalgic way, or in retreat from the challenges of the present, but to inspire "a bold emergence into tomorrow".[8]

The hand of fellowship

After the teaching comes fellowship (*koinonia*) in the four characteristics of the community described by Luke. We have already looked at the lengths the apostles went to at the Council of Jerusalem around AD 50 to preserve the fellowship when it came to theological disputes. In Paul's account of the aftermath of that Council, although he is somewhat dismissive of "those who were supposed to be acknowledged leaders" (Galatians 2:6), he reports that James and Cephas "gave to Barnabas and me the right hand of fellowship" (Galatians 2:9). Paul may not have much time for the leadership, but he does recognise the bond which keeps them in partnership. There is an interesting footnote to that episode which takes us back to one of our central concerns: "They asked only one thing, that we remember the poor" (Galatians 2:10).

Fellowship should be evident at all levels in the Church, not just on the abstract level of doctrinal dispute. The force of *koinonia* is relational and if Christian communities are not marked by a certain quality of relationships then they surely do not deserve the name. Sociologists tell us that identity is initiated, sustained and developed in a community, so with faith. You won't last long alone. There is a palpable excitement in the way Luke describes the life of the early community and how people behaved: "They would sell their possessions and goods and distribute the proceeds to all, as any had need. Day by day, as they spent much time together in the temple, they broke bread at home and ate their food with glad and generous hearts, praising God and having the goodwill of all the people" (Acts 2:45-47).

There is, of course, something idyllic about this description. Anyone who has lived in or around a Christian community for more than five minutes knows that the reality is somewhat more mixed. In the early Church also there is certainly no suggestion that this state of bliss was sustained for very long. In a number of Paul's letters there are references to disputes and disgraceful behaviour. Paul is not backwards about coming forwards when he is not happy. You can almost see the abashed faces of the Corinthians who gathered together to read this letter: "I am not writing this to make you ashamed, but to admonish you as my beloved children" (1 Corinthians 4:14). We have been working on fellowship from the very beginning, getting it right, getting it badly wrong, but always inspired by a vision of *communio* which finds one of its finest expressions in the writings of Saint John Paul II (see Gems #10).

The singing of psalms and hymns, or "the prayers" (Acts 2:42), was another of the four characteristics of the community described by Luke. In his highly informative set of talks on the early Church[9] Raymond Brown goes into detail on each of the four, but in relation to the prayers he makes the point that the earliest Christians would have prayed as they had prayed as Jews, since that was their prayer tradition. In Luke's Gospel he finds echoes and extracts of Jewish payers, such as Mary's Magnificat which closely resembles the praise song of Samuel's mother, Hannah, in the Old Testament (see Luke 1:46-55; 1 Samuel 2:1-10). But very quickly the Christian community started to

Gems from the Treasure Box #10

A spirituality of communion indicates above all the heart's contemplation of the mystery of the Trinity dwelling in us, and whose light we must also be able to see shining on the face of the brothers and sisters around us. This makes us able to share their joys and sufferings, to sense their desires and attend to their needs, to offer them deep and genuine friendship. A spirituality of communion implies also the ability to see what is positive in others, to welcome it and prize it as a gift from God: not only as a gift for the brother or sister who has received it directly, but also as a "gift for me".

A spirituality of communion means, finally, to know how to "make room" for our brothers and sisters, bearing "each other's burdens" (*Gal* 6:2) and resisting the selfish temptations which constantly beset us and provoke competition, careerism, distrust and jealousy.

Saint John Paul II,
Novo Millennio Ineunte

compose and use its own explicitly Christian prayers. The most famous example is the Our Father, the Lord's Prayer, which can be found in two different versions in the Gospels of Matthew (6:9-13) and Luke (11:1-4). Perhaps the earliest was the hymn contained in Paul's letter to the Philippians, believed to have been written as early as AD 52. Scholars believe Paul lifted the hymn directly into his letter. It is an invitation to have the same mind as Christ Jesus:

> who, though he was in the form of God,
> did not regard equality with God
> as something to be exploited,
> but emptied himself,
> taking the form of a slave,
> being born in human likeness.
> And being found in human form,
> he humbled himself
> and became obedient to the point of death –
> even death on a cross.
> Therefore God also highly exalted him
> and gave him the name that is above every
>   name. (2:6-10)

It is remarkable to consider that less than twenty years after the death and resurrection of Jesus the first Christians had such a powerful theology (or Christology) of the significance of the life and death of Jesus (unless the hymn was added later which some scholars believe, but it is still almost certainly from the first century). What strikes me most, and seems to me to be the pattern of the Christian journey, is the focus on "emptied himself" (*kenosis*). Jesus really did keep nothing for himself or of himself. He reveals a God of vulnerability and non-violence. He submitted himself to the very depth of human emptying and then was raised high. There is something about the type of death Jesus suffered which is central to Christian belief. As Raymond Brown says in his recorded talks on the early Church, Jesus could have died of a heart attack or a virus in Jerusalem and still have been raised to glory by his Father. The abject nature of his death, the abysmal nature of the blood-letting and humiliation, is part of the mystery. God in Jesus not only descended to the very depths of human suffering, but also revealed complete powerlessness in being fixed to the cross.

This is our God, the crucifixion tells us, and this is the path we have to follow. Not literally, we should say immediately. The Church is now very clear that self-inflicted suffering is not encouraged (see *Gaudium et Spes*, 14). The path of the Christian, of those who follow Jesus, is a path of emptying oneself of what we are taught to consider important and surrendering ourselves to loving service of God and neighbour. It is an invitation to surrender all addictions to power and control in order to be "reborn" in the transformation of the resurrection. It is also worth saying, lest we cause those on the threshold to take fright, that this is the work of a lifetime. For some it is dramatic and convulsive but for most disciples it is a long road with many diversions.

The fourth characteristic was the "breaking of bread" which is also about giving. We saw earlier in Luke's account of the Last Supper how Jesus said to his disciples that the bread was his body given "for you" (Luke 22:19). I have heard many people who have left the Church say that the one thing they miss most is the Eucharist (or Mass, as many people would say).

The Church often reaches the highest expressions of poetry and authority when talking about this subject. In the *Catechism of the Catholic Church*, the Eucharist is described as "the source and summit of the Christian life… For in the blessed Eucharist is contained the whole spiritual good of the Church, namely Christ himself."[10] For two thousand years the Mass or Eucharist has been a place of encounter between Christ and the disciple. It has also been the battleground for the most damaging and divisive of disputes. In the Catholic culture described in earlier chapters the Mass was something of a performance. Something important was happening up at the holy end and the congregation were mere spectators. At the heart of this was transformation: bread and wine becoming the body and blood of Christ. Very often this removed any pressure on the spectators to be transformed themselves.

In the synoptic Gospels, the accounts of the Last Supper all include what are known as "the words of institution"; when Jesus invites his disciples to take the bread and wine which are his body and blood given for them and keep doing this in his memory. At least in that respect we've done as he asked. These are the words Mass-goers are familiar with at the consecration. But John in his Gospel account of the Last Supper does not use the words of institution. Instead, he relates the story of how Jesus took off his outer garment and washed the feet of his disciples, despite objections from Peter. Some scholars have speculated that by the time he came to write his Gospel disputes over the meaning of the Eucharist had caused division in his community and, guided by the Beloved Disciple, he wanted to get to the heart of what the Eucharist was about. The Church always uses this account at the Mass on Holy Thursday, the feast that celebrates the institution of the Eucharist. So what is going on in John's Gospel? How can the washing of the feet take us to the heart of this sacrament?

Ronald Rolheiser provides a compelling commentary on this episode and, indeed, many other aspects of the Eucharist in *Our One Great Act of Fidelity*:

> It is a call to move from worship to service, to take the nourishment, the embrace, the kiss, we have just received from God and the community and translate it immediately and directly into loving service of others. To take the Eucharist seriously is to begin to wash the feet of others, especially the feet of the poor and those with whom we struggle most relationally.[11]

The Eucharist is not some private devotion, or a spectacle for our spiritual enthralment. It is not a "prize for the perfect"[12], as Pope Francis says, but nourishment for the weak so that we will not leave feeling better about ourselves but a little more transformed into the kind of people who will not walk past the suffering neighbour or hide behind the outer garments of pride and correctness, but will get on our knees and minister to the needs of a hurting world. To proclaim our faith is important, but it is not enough. In Luke's Gospel Jesus reminds us that his brothers and sisters are "those who hear the word of God and do it" (Luke 8:20).

Comments from the twelve on Church and community

I believe in the Holy Spirit and the baptism of the Holy Spirit. The Holy Spirit gives you the power and the understanding of what salvation and Christ is all about and when I got involved with the Holy Spirit that's when I really understood as well Christ in me; understood and accepted and started living a life as a Christian and wanting to be a disciple of Christ. When you go into the charismatic movement within the Catholic Church you see people, they look like Protestants really, they are amazing people, they are zealots, they live life, they are full of the life of God because the Holy Spirit is alive in them, they are aware of him. He is God on earth. You need to understand who the Holy Spirit really is.

Emiliana, 45, charity co-founder

Sometimes our sandwich or our snack that we brought to school, we'd give half of it to the needy for the free school in the evening for the poor girls, because we used to have the free school there and we would see them. It was part of always giving part of what you have, at the same time we were taught to appreciate what you have, the blessings that you have and the need to share. I grew up with that kind of Church. I was surrounded by religious people who carried on that kind of way of being a Catholic and later on when things became quite difficult with martial law. I had a sister who was a political detainee and so we would go to where she was detained. In the detention area were priests who were also detained and we were allowed to have Mass and it would be so meaningful because it's a small group and we would just have bread, a big piece of bread that we'd break, and we are part of it and you know that everyone is going through difficult times and that's the time that we all get together.

It was a very good celebration of the Eucharist because each would have their own problems, their own issues and they're in a detention centre where anything can happen to them, including my sister, and yet everyone was there to celebrate the Eucharist and the hope is always there. Usually every Sunday when you would have Mass in the centre, sisters would come over, guests, friends would come over so it becomes a bigger community and you know you're not alone. There're just so many taking care of you or being aware that you are in this kind of situation.

Rebecca, 51, Dean of Studies

It has a social meaning in the sense that the Church is that space where you can have your personal prayer but, for example, for overseas workers, that's where you also meet your co-Filipinos. You can establish identity in a strange country and it keeps them on an even keel as long as they can go to Church. It has a faith dimension but it also has a social function. In fact, when some of the students have plans working abroad I always advise them: "Make sure you go to church on Sunday because that's your only way to connect with other Filipinos who are there and for somebody to know that you're there," because sometimes they do not register in the embassy or in the consulate. So they know that you left the country but they don't know where you are and if anything happens at least there's a record if someone's going to look for you, especially with many Filipinos who go undocumented or go with fake documents. The Church has provided that particular space where they can be with others. In the Philippines the Church also performs a function, it's the centre where people come together to pray, it's the place where they can do their devotion but it's also a social space and your sense of belonging.

Mary John, 78, nun

I think it's a bit of a family-tree-type thing. You've got your local physical church with that community but it represents something much more global and that's really exciting because everyone's faith is a little bit different and I think the Church for me definitely isn't just a physical thing, I see it as being something that brings together people that otherwise are quite different and gives them a common ground and gives them something to seek comfort in when times are difficult. You've already got this idea that God is some kind of figure up in the sky and that's really hard to process and comprehend so drawing it closer and closer in really helps me to make the Church a personal thing. The Church sounds very institutional but I think that actually as a community it's a lot less formal and that for me is what became quite important, especially recently, over the last couple of years.

Xita, 20, student

The last thing I would say about discipleship relates back to the tensions in our own Church and this is brought out by Francis in *Evangelii Gaudium*, which is: if we don't actually have joy in each other, they don't have to agree with us, they don't have to be of the same view as us, but we have to be able to form community. So in that sense the key part of discipleship is actually having a community where joy, forgiveness, exchange takes place. That really counts today – families are breaking up, communities are breaking up.

In [my city] the church that I know best that has a kind of welcome where you feel "gosh, there's a community here, I could become part of it" is the Evangelical church down the road. When they meet, all the parking is taken up in this area and their services are teeming with people. Why? Because when you go there, there is a welcome, there is an integration into a community and suddenly being Christian is not just a part-time Sunday affair. You talk to people who go there and they're really thinking about what it is to be a Christian all the time. Whereas we have this mindset, because of our Sunday obligation history, that being a Catholic is about turning up on Sunday and ticking off a checklist of beliefs. So in a way we've got a lot to learn.

Greg, 56, university teacher

Reflections for individuals

- In your journal recollect any occasions when you've made a public declaration about belief or commitment – what did it mean to you?

- Reflect on the communities you belong to – which are the most important for you?

- Have you thought about joining or rejoining a Catholic/Christian community – who might you go to for advice or encouragement?

Reflection activity for groups

- In what ways does your Christian community practise the four characteristics described by Luke: the apostles' teaching, fellowship, breaking of the bread and the prayers? Is that a useful template for evaluation or community renewal? When was the last time your community read the Acts of the Apostles looking for inspiration from the early Church?

Resources for further study

Raymond E. Brown, *The Beginnings of the Church.* Six CD Set (Penley: Welcome Recordings, 2005). Known as a charming and engaging lecturer, Raymond E. Brown could convey scholarly points in a way that could be understood. I would describe him as a pastoral scholar who speaks always out of his own deep faith with a view to how knowledge of the scriptures and the Church might form the faith of the modern disciple.

Raymond E. Brown, *The Churches the Apostles Left Behind* (New York: Paulist Press, 1984). He regarded this in many ways as his best book. It is so readable and informative about the key communities of the early Church and has many applications for the Church today.

Pheme Perkins, *Reading the New Testament* (New York: Paulist Press, 2012). A comprehensive and informed introduction to all the books and major themes of the New Testament.

YouCat: Youth Catechism of the Catholic Church (San Francisco: Ignatius Press, 2011). This is the catechism of the Church, with the official stamp of approval from Benedict XVI, but presented in a very engaging way, with a wealth of quotations and prayers as well as "translations" of the catechism. When it says "youth", it doesn't really mean just young people. I think it would suit honest searchers of any age.

Notes

[1] Raymond E. Brown, *101 Questions on the Bible* (New Jersey: Paulist Press, 1990), 110

[2] Brown, *101 Questions on the Bible,* 110

[3] Walter Kasper, *Pope Francis' Revolution of Tenderness and Love* (New Jersey: Paulist Press, 2015), 28

[4] Raniero Cantalamessa, http://www.news.va/en/news/fourth-lenten-reflection-by-fr-raniero-cantalamess, accessed 3 January 2015

[5] Raniero Cantalamessa, http://www.wcr.ab.ca/WCRThisWeek/Stories/tabid/61/entryid/984/Default.aspx, accessed 3 January 2015

[6] Sherry A. Weddell, *Forming Intentional Disciples* (Huntington: Our Sunday Visitor, 2012), 67

[7] Pope Francis, *Evangelii Gaudium* [The Joy of the Gospel], 164

[8] Kasper, *Pope Francis' Revolution of Tenderness and Love,* 27

[9] Raymond E. Brown, *The Beginnings of the Church,* 6 CD Set (Penley: Welcome Recordings, 2005)

[10] *Catechism of the Catholic Church,* 1324, http://www.vatican.va/archive/ccc_css/archive/catechism/p2s2c1a3.htm, accessed 1 February 2015

[11] Ronald Rolheiser, *Our One Great Act of Fidelity: Waiting for Christ in the Eucharist* (New York: Doubleday, 2011),

[12] Pope Francis, *Evangelii Gaudium,* 13

Bruised and hurting – the Church today and the role of the laity

The numbers of converts excitedly reported by Luke in the Acts of the Apostles kept on growing over the next three centuries, despite periodic Roman persecution. No other religion in the classical world at this time had the same dynamic hold over the imagination of people, especially the poor. Estimates vary, but by the beginning of the fourth century the population of the Christian Church was anything from four to six million. Future growth was all but guaranteed when the Emperor Constantine agreed the Edict of Milan with his rival Licinius in AD 313. Christians would henceforth be treated with benevolence within the Roman Empire. A few decades later Theodosius I decreed that all citizens should be Christian and the transformation from a ragged band of itinerant preachers to cultural dominance was complete.

Whether that was a good thing or not has been argued about ever since. When a religion is official, with the mechanisms of state to back it up, it will usually spend a good deal of energy suppressing versions of itself which are not official. A few years before Theodosius came to power, the first major ecumenical council in Nicaea, convened by Constantine around 325, defined the doctrine of the divinity of Christ ("consubstantial with the Father…"). Those who found themselves on the wrong side of this dogma, like the followers of Arius, had more than disapproving sermons to worry about. For the first time, the army was on the side of Jesus, which does not sit comfortably with the figure from the Gospels we looked at in Chapter 2. The poor, healing, humble Jesus did not give any indication that this was the kind of kingdom he wanted. In fact, as we saw in Luke's temptations in the wilderness, the urge to temporal power was rejected as a distortion of the kingdom.

There has often been a tendency in the Church for the needs of the institution to overshadow the spirit of Jesus, the inspiration for the institution. The historian Géza Vermes argues that after Nicaea "membership of the Church primarily depended on adherence to the Nicene Creed. Intellectual assent to dogma gained precedence over the heart's openness to charisma urged by the historical Jesus".[1] Many throughout the Christian era have paid the ultimate price for being on the wrong side of dogma. In recent times the price was less physically painful but still, if you adhered to the wrong doctrine, you could be "silenced" or forbidden to teach in a church institution. In Chapter 4 we looked at the importance of being on message in order to avoid endless disagreements and splinter groups. There were times when the need for unity, and therefore authority, took precedence and at those times the open invitation of the *kerygma* and the call to personal encounter were sometimes lost in what sounded like the uncompromising voice of dogma.

In the fourth century, with increasingly well-defined conditions for membership and the full backing of the civil authorities in the West, the Christian Church grew exponentially, despite the collapse of the Roman Empire. The Reformation in the sixteenth century saw major splits in the Church, but the age of exploration saw new mission fields open up in the Americas, Africa and Asia. The invitation to convert was often encouraged at the end of a musket, which was a world away from the passionate witness of the apostles, but by whatever means the numbers kept growing. By 1910, according to the Pew Research Center, the number of Catholics worldwide had reached 291 million,[2] which was about half of all Christians and seventeen per cent of the world's total population. By 2010, the number of Catholics had risen to 1.1 billion, but remarkably those percentages remained about the same. In other words, in 2010 as one hundred years earlier, the Catholic population accounted for around half of the global population of Christians and sixteen per cent of the total global population.

What has changed quite dramatically in the last hundred years is the geographic distribution of the world's Catholics. In 1910, Europe was home to around sixty-five per cent of all Catholics, with around twenty-five per cent living in Latin America and the Caribbean. In 2010, the figure in Europe had dropped to twenty-four per cent and the figure in Latin America and the Caribbean had risen to nearly forty per cent. In that context, the election of a pope in 2013 from Latin America makes good sense and the trend in those figures suggests that future popes may also come from Latin America or sub-Saharan Africa, where the Catholic population has risen from just over one million in 1910 to 170 million, or sixteen per cent of the global Catholic total, by 2010. The fact that Pope Francis has gone outside of Europe for many of his new cardinals (the electors of popes) suggests that this will be the future direction of the Church's leadership.

Those who regard the numbers game as a measure of success might be somewhat pleased by such figures.

That is a lot of Catholics after all. Common sense, however, should introduce some cautionary notes. The 2010 figures, for example, suggest that there are nearly 50 million Catholics in Italy. I have had the good fortune to visit Italy a number of times and any Sunday Masses I have attended there, apart from in Saint Peter's Square, do not suggest that anything like all of the 50 million Catholics are in regular attendance, but rather a few elderly covered heads dotted around the Church. Italy – like Spain, France, Ireland, southern Germany and Poland – is a traditionally Catholic European country; a traditional Catholic culture like the one described in Chapter 1. But the reality is that Mass attendance and vocations to the priesthood have fallen sharply in the last thirty to forty years, and it will take more than one charismatic pope to reverse that trend.

The picture is even less encouraging in the new powerhouses of Latin America. A major Pew Research Center study examined religious affiliations, beliefs and practices in eighteen countries across Latin America and the Caribbean. The findings are troubling for the number crunchers. The report says: "In nearly every country surveyed, the Catholic Church has experienced net losses from religious switching, as many Latin Americans have joined evangelical Protestant churches or rejected organized religion altogether."[3] Some national level examples are striking: roughly one in four Nicaraguans and one in five Brazilians are former Catholics. How can we explain this phenomenon? If the Catholic Church proclaims the compelling revelation of God as lived by Jesus, why on earth are so many people going elsewhere to hear it? And it is happening quickly. In most of the countries surveyed at least a third of current Protestants were raised in the Catholic Church.

118

A personal encounter

The main reason given in the survey takes us right back to where we started. Of the eight possible explanations for switching offered on the survey, the most frequently cited was that those who left the Catholic Church for a Protestant Church did so because they were seeking a more personal connection with God. The second most cited reason was that they enjoyed the style of worship at the new church more. The survey found that Protestants are more observant than Catholics, pray more often than Catholics and are more likely to read scripture outside of religious services (although this is often a literal or fundamentalist reading, which includes a belief that Jesus will return in their lifetime, not the kind of reading we were describing in Chapter 2). Many of the new Protestants belong to Pentecostal churches, where services often include divine healing, speaking in tongues and direct revelations from God. It is a far cry from my little parish church in rural England where my hands only leave my side to make the sign of the cross, or to receive Holy Communion.

Timothy Radcliffe comments on the phenomenon of Pentecostalism and recognises that it is fast becoming the latest deep division to trouble the Christian family. The problem, he admits, is that if we in the Catholic Church say we receive the Spirit at baptism and confirmation, then why does nothing happen, why do most people in Catholic churches seem half-asleep? In contrast, the Pentecostal churches are a movement of "enormous vitality which is transforming the lives of millions. Its expansion in mainland China is phenomenal. It attracts people because here one can see the power of the

Spirit at work. Part of its success in Latin America is in healing broken families, getting men off drink and stopping them beating their wives, thus enabling them to climb out of poverty."[4] As Greg comments at the end of the previous chapter, the evangelical communities have a powerful sense of welcome and purpose. People in these churches are obsessed with being Christians *as a lifestyle*, not as carrying a card that needs to be stamped once a week. There is adult commitment, just as there was in those very early days; and baptism in the Spirit, just as there was in those Spirit-filled days.

The Catholic culture which has prevailed since the Council of Trent (1545-1563) was a predominantly sacramental system run by a cadre of highly educated celibate men for the spiritual benefit of a largely uneducated mass membership. I do not wish in any way to detract from the pastoral work of many good priests over many years, but I do want to consider the impact of this phase of the life of the Church on the spiritual growth (or not) of its members. You were baptised as a child and "conversion" in adulthood was not seen to be necessary, although it did occasionally happen. As we heard Gerard W. Hughes say in Chapter 1, the formation of the faithful often stopped at the level of childhood, as Paul also comments at the end of the chapter.

Despite the changes brought in by Vatican II the Church has not fundamentally changed its structure or its approach to formation. There is now a much more educated and enquiring congregation and there is simply not the capacity to engage them in the grown-up formation that is such a feature of the resurgent Protestant churches. There is not the same culture of supporting and encouraging active adult Christians in the Catholic Church, or what Sherry Weddell calls *intentional disciples*. She has many years of experience in parish evangelisation and is in no doubt about what the future holds unless we wake up to this great shift:

> If this trend does not change, in ten years it will cease to matter that we have a priest shortage… Sacramental practise will plummet at a rate that will make the post-Vatican II era

look good, and the Church's financial support will vanish... So let's be clear: *In the twenty-first century, cultural Catholicism is dead as a retention strategy, because God has no grandchildren. In the twenty-first century, we have to foster intentional Catholicism rather than cultural Catholicism.*[5]

Weddell identifies "two tracks" which seem to define the typical Catholic approach to the spiritual life: either "ordinary Catholic" or "saint" (see Gems from the Treasure Box # 11; Rahner seems to believe that only the latter will last into the future). That does ring true from my own experience in the Church. Those who showed a more than "ordinary" interest in prayer, scripture or Christian living were seen as a bit embarrassing, either a complete chancer or a genuine saint. The totally Catholic culture didn't always know what to do with an intentional disciple on a journey of faith to becoming more like Christ. In the course of her "Making Disciples" seminars in 2004, Weddell asked parish leaders in over sixty dioceses in America what was the approximate percentage of their parishioners they would describe as intentional disciples. She was astonished by the consistency of the response: about *five per cent.*

The Church is on the verge of a new era, when the assent and observance of previous years, which may have produced Catholics but not always Christians, is giving way to a new era of rediscovering the source of the Christian movement, Jesus Christ, and what it means to regard him as your personal Lord and Saviour and to follow in his footsteps. That kind of talk can make some traditionalists nervous, if they think that church teaching is being diluted or ignored. Nobody is saying that, but the insight that is breaking through in so many ways is that doctrinal adherence and sacramental observance are no guarantee of an encounter with the living God and will not transform you or transform society to be more like the kingdom of God. Richard Rohr reminds us of the truth hidden in plain sight:

> The fact that the two great wars emerged in a Christian Europe filled with Churches and theology schools needs to be examined. The fact that racism, profound social inequality and anti-Semitism were not recognised as a serious problem until almost two thousand years after Jesus is forever a judgement on the immaturity of western Christianity, whether Catholic or Protestant.[6]

It seems undeniable to me that many people who claimed to be Catholic or Christian were in fact completely untouched, or *untransformed*, by such an allegiance. There are many who have waged war, or, as Rohr says, supported oppressive or racist regimes and structures right up to the present day, while at the same time calling themselves Catholic. That seems to me to lie at the heart of this burning issue: to be a disciple of Jesus means to be on a journey of transformation into one who is more loving of God and neighbour. Was that not the way that Jesus showed us? And yet, despite the big numbers, so few seem to be really interested in walking through this "narrow gate". It is so much easier in some ways to live by the operative values of society, to be nice to those around us but to be fundamentally selfish, to do what we can to advance ourselves in the world and to enjoy the arrangements of our pleasures. Who wants this alternative low road of humility? If that is the true path then why were we born with all this drive, concupiscence and cunning? It seems like major spiritual surgery, or, as we said earlier, *metanoia*.

Gems from the Treasure Box #11

The devout Christian of the future will either be a "mystic" – one who has experienced "something" – or he will cease to be anything at all.

Karl Rahner,
Christians Living Formerly and Today

Priest, prophet and king

I do not wish to give the impression that the Church has only recently rediscovered the Gospel message of Jesus. That would be a travesty and an injustice to the many "ordinary saints" in every age who "get it" and who live good and godly lives. But it is true to say that it is only recently that the Church has had anything to say about the majority of its membership as a group. The laity, as we are called, was not the subject of any specific declarations from any council to my knowledge until Vatican II. As we heard in Chapter 1, the posture of the laity tended to be passive and obedient, child-like. There were certainly many lay associations and groups in the history of the Church doing good works (and the numbers today are growing) but there were no documents about the theology of the laity until *Lumen Gentium* in 1964.

In Chapter 1 we looked briefly at the progress of *Lumen Gentium* (*LG*) through the Council sessions of 1963–1964 and we focused in particular on the expansive biblical language used to describe the Church, which replaced the more academic and juridical language of previous generations. The description of the laity likewise reveals a striking new approach. The document speaks of the "common dignity" (*LG*, 32) of the members of the Church and asserts that there is "no inequality in Christ and in the church" (*LG*, 32). This seemed like a radical departure from the hierarchical Church when the role of the laity at the bottom of the pyramid was to "pray, pay, obey". By baptism, the laity are "made sharers in Christ's priestly, prophetic and royal office" (*LG*, 31) whose special vocation is to "seek the kingdom of God by engaging in temporal affairs and ordering them in accordance with the will of God" (*LG*, 31). If the role of the Church, through the action of the Spirit, is to transform the world according to the kingdom of God as revealed by Jesus, then the laity has a key role to play. We are, after all, on the front line, right in the middle of the mess and muddle of the world.

The offices of priest, prophet and king do seem somewhat remote from the Jesus we looked at in Chapter 2. We need good teachers to help us understand what these offices mean and how exactly we share in them. Timothy Radcliffe offers a helpful definition of each. We think of priests in the sacramental Church many of us have been brought up in, but Radcliffe reminds us that Jesus was not a priest like the priests of his day, making temple offerings for the atonement of sin. "His priesthood is to be the mediator between God and humanity. He embodied God's love for us, and our love of God. His only sacrifice was his self-offering."[7] To share in this priesthood is to live a life of self-offering love, not in an abstract heaven-oriented sense, but by mediating God's love to those nearest to us, those we work with, those remote from us, and above all those whom we find unlovable. That is how the world will be "transformed" and saved from the darkness of sin and violence.

A prophet is not one who can foretell the future but one who speaks God's word. Radcliffe says that "the vocation of every human being is prophetic, to speak fertile words that nourish people and make them strong."[8] It is a ministry we exercise every day in how we speak to each other, especially those whose role in life is centred on words: teachers, writers, journalists, campaigners, politicians. Our prophetic role is to speak words that are true, that enliven others and do not crush them. Prophets can also challenge and denounce, but not with contempt. Indeed, *Lumen Gentium* encourages the laity to speak out when all is not what it should be in the Church: "They have the right and indeed sometimes the duty to make known their opinion on matters which concern the good of the Church" (*LG*, 37). The Church has not always provided the means for these voices to be heard but that does not diminish the duty to speak out.

In recent times, there was much to speak out against. It seemed at one point as if every day fresh allegations of child abuse were emerging and the Church was transfixed by the sins of its members. I remember the profound embarrassment of my parents when these allegations came into the public domain. When we were children watching television together and an overly affectionate scene came on, my father would rustle behind his newspaper and say: "Is there nothing else on?" As adults, on those few occasions when we sat together with the television on and the news brought painful revelations for the Church, my father used the same line. My parents' generation simply did not criticise the Church. It was the fault of aggressive media, a modernist plot. That argument has weakened in the face of overwhelming evidence and the Church is now slowly trying to deal properly with the crimes of its members, but only because a few brave ones spoke out.

Jesus was an unlikely king. In his public death nailed to a cross, he was mocked as "the King of the Jews" in Hebrew, Greek and Latin (John 19:20). He inverted notions of kingship and power. His kingship was "not of this world" and was exercised by refusing violence and following the path of powerlessness. Radcliffe comments that we share this kingship "in the non-violent ways in which we share in decision-making in our society and Church".[9] There is a special dimension of this office for all those involved in any form of government, indeed any role which involves the use of resources. We are all called to be stewards of the common good, according to our gifts and role in life. *Lumen Gentium* is unambiguous in its call for the laity to work for "a more equitable distribution" (*LG*, 36) of the goods of creation and more than that to take an active part in improving "structures and conditions which constitute an inducement to sin" (*LG*, 36). If we can easily forget the radical message of the Gospel, we can also very quickly lose the power of these Council documents.

A face of Christ

A fine example of Christian kingship would be Jun Lozada, a remarkable man I had the good fortune to meet and interview as one of the twelve on a visit to the Philippines. Jun was a successful corporate man in Manila: bright, wealthy, well liked and blessed with family. He could have stayed that way and ended his days in one of the guarded, gated communities for the rich on the outskirts of Manila. He knew, like everybody else in business in the Philippines, that corruption was endemic but then he was involved with one government contract in which the scale of corruption was so shocking that he decided to become a whistle-blower and speak out for truth and justice. It was remarkably brave and led to months of harassment, investigations and eventually a convenient relocation to London, away from his wife and children. In the meantime a warrant was issued for his arrest and his trial began.

He could have stayed away and let "justice" run its course but he chose to return to Manila to clear his name. He was arrested after taking just a few steps onto the tarmac and didn't even get to immigration. He said he had been "kidnapped in the middle of a busy airport and only the powerful ones can do that". His wife was waiting for him, supported by some Dominican priests. When I asked him what was going to happen to him he replied calmly: "I was going to be killed." He was being driven to a well-known killing field south of Manila. It was thanks to the Dominicans that his wife got on to live radio and pleaded for his life. Such was the uproar in the media that the men in shades in the car were told to turn around and bring him back. He was far from safe, of course, and it was another religious order, the Christian Brothers, who gave him and his family sanctuary for the next five years while he continued to speak the truth to power.

However, his encounters with the church were mixed. He was astonished when one very senior church leader in Manila offered him his current salary and a house if he dropped the case and handed over his papers. In that meeting there was one other person, a nun, who simply made a *No* gesture to him with her index finger. He also remembers that she managed to eat all the biscuits. He left that meeting and never saw the churchman again. I referred above to the child abuse cases which rocked the Church. In the Ryan Report (2009), which detailed the abuses of children in the "industrial schools" in Ireland in the second half of the twentieth century, the Christian Brothers were named and shamed on many occasions. In the case of Jun Lozada they were the face of Christ to a family in dire need. This is the Church, in its darkness and light, in all its original sin and original blessing. How could it be otherwise when it is populated by human beings?

Gems from the Treasure Box #12

When someone experiences laughter or tears, bears responsibility, stands by the truth, breaks through the egoism in his life with other people; when someone hopes against hope, faces the shallowness and stupidity of the daily rush and bustle with humour and patience, refusing to be embittered; when someone learns to be silent and in this inner silence lets the evil in his heart die rather than spread outward; in a word, whenever someone lives as he would like to live, combating his own egoism and the continual temptation to inner despair – there is an event of grace.

Karl Rahner,
Secular Life and the Sacraments

One dogmatic certainty

Morale in the Church is very hard to determine. It depends on who you ask and what Catholic newspapers, if any, you read. Pollsters are not much interested in asking the question. But speaking from my own experience, the morale of many people in the Church was very low towards the end of the papacy of Benedict XVI. He fully understood that people were leaving the Church looking for that sense of personal encounter, and convened a Synod in 2012 on the New Evangelisation. In the *Lineamenta*, or preparatory document published before the Synod, we hear the call to encounter, which was often a feature of Benedict's papacy:

> Being Christian is not the result of an ethical choice or a lofty idea, but the encounter with an event, a person, which gives life a new horizon and a decisive direction. Since God has first loved us (cf. Jn 4:10), love is now no longer a mere "command"; it is the response to the gift of love with which God draws near to us.[10]

The message was clear, but it was largely lost in the anxiety of the final years of Benedict's reign. The Church seemed more preoccupied with its own problems, not just the ongoing issue of how to respond adequately to the abuse cases, but the growing concerns over Vatican finances and the so-called VatiLeaks scandal of 2012, in which stolen and leaked documents, including personal papers of the Pope, allegedly revealed corruption and blackmail in the Vatican. Walter Kasper, a cardinal with an intimate knowledge of the workings of the Church, says that the problem went deeper than the shocks of abuse scandals and crisis in the Roma Curia:

"Additionally, there arose the impression of mental fatigue and exhaustion, a lack of confidence and enthusiasm. The church was increasingly preoccupied with itself… Its prophetic powers appeared extinguished and its missionary vitality appeared to languish."[11] The cardinal is articulating what many felt at the time. It was a low point. There are many who believe that the stress of all this was responsible for Benedict's decision to resign as Pope in 2013.

Gems from the Treasure Box #13

To Martin Luther, who reproached him for remaining in the Catholic Church in spite of its corruption, Erasmus of Rotterdam answered in a letter: "I bear with this Church in the hope that it will improve, just as it is obliged to bear with me in the hope that I will improve."

Raniero Cantalamessa,
from the conference
"Nothing More Beautiful", May 2011

The Church had a new Pope in March 2013 and almost immediately we were hearing a new kind of voice. The same teaching, but delivered with a candour, humility and humour we simply were not used to hearing from the balcony of Saint Peter's. This was the first non-European Pope for 1,300 years, the first Pope from Latin America, the first Jesuit Pope and the first Francis. In his first apostolic exhortation, "The Joy of the Gospel", we hear the same call as from Benedict to "a renewed personal encounter with Jesus Christ".[12] That message is accompanied by another theme which has become something of a defining motif for Francis: the mercy of God. Writing in *The Tablet*, Fr Daniel O'Leary says that: "His [Francis'] commitment to a Church of mercy springs from his 'one dogmatic certainty' – that every single person, without exception, is the home of God." [13]

The great appeal of Francis is that he does not only preach the word of God but he speaks it in his actions, he embraces people as if this "one dogmatic certainty"was a daily reality, as if in fact he was embracing Christ in everybody he meets. Every pope, every Christian, will have their own slightly different version of the *kerygma*, the summary of the life and mission of Jesus which is the first call to those on the threshold of discipleship. Pope Francis offers us a *kerygma* which foregrounds the mercy and tenderness of Jesus, a consistent feature of all the Gospel accounts of his life. He invites us to consider a discipleship which is all about ministering to people. At times in the life of the Church, and the life of the disciple whether intentional or not, we can lose sight of the needs of our brothers and sisters right in front of us and become overly concerned with the cerebral, the intellectual, the external manifestations of ritual and observance. Francis brings us back to the heart of an incarnational faith. He reminds us that we also encounter Christ in the suffering body of our neighbour.

Francis applies a humble but steely consistency to this message. He does not just say things like this and ignore the structures and behaviour in the Church which say the opposite. He is not afraid to criticise those in the Church who have an "ostentatious preoccupation with the liturgy" (*EG*, 95) or who "remain intransigently faithful to a particular Catholic style from the past" (*EG*, 94) or who exhibit "narcissistic and authoritarian elitism" (*EG*, 94) instead of opening the door to grace. If Jun Lozada is a fine example of the exercise of Christian kingship, then Francis is an example of the exercise of the Christian office of prophet. It is as if he wants to consign the worst elements of the totally Catholic culture to history and introduce a new era of discipleship more truly based on the heart of the Gospel. And he doesn't stop with general criticisms of the excesses of a clerical culture. He also deals head-on with the Church's responsibility for Christ-like governance by telling the Roman Curia (the Vatican government) face to face that they are sick.

In another remarkable moment in his papacy, Francis spoke to the assembled representatives of the Curia in the splendour of the Clementine Hall in the Vatican on 22 December 2014. Having wished everybody a happy Christmas he then went on to outline fifteen "diseases" which afflicted the body of the Church's government. The list includes thinking they were immortal, excessive busyness, mental and spiritual "petrification", excessive planning, spiritual Alzheimer's, rivalry and vainglory, gossiping, grumbling, backbiting, indifference to others, a lugubrious face and hoarding.[14] Apparently there was light applause when the Pope had finished. Nobody had ever spoken like this before to the Roman Curia, in public. A revolution of tenderness clearly required some new thinking from those in charge.

In the wider world it led to descriptions of Francis as a "turnaround CEO", the kind of chief executive who is capable of transformational leadership. He has said himself that because of his age and health his might be a short papacy but it would be difficult for his successor to embark on any other path than the one Francis has mapped out for the Church. He has brought a perspective from Latin America which many of us in Europe did not encounter through the papacies of John Paul II and Benedict XVI. Few in the West had ever heard of the Aparecida Document which Francis quotes from in "The Joy of the Gospel". This document was the outcome of the Fifth General Conference of the Latin American and Caribbean Bishops in 2007 at Aparecida in Brazil, home of the Basilica of Our Lady of Aparecida and one of the most popular sites of religious pilgrimage in Latin America. The thinking emerging from that document is very much about a missionary church encounter with the poor, taking the Church on to the streets.

This is what informs the call of Francis for a Church "which is bruised, hurting and dirty because it has been out on the streets, rather than a Church which is unhealthy from being confined and from clinging to its own security" (EG, 49). This is the message which the tired Church in Europe needed to hear. Open your doors, leave the security of your sacred space and go out and make contact with people who are hungry for meaning and a goal in life. This after all is what we find in the Gospels. Most of the preaching of Jesus took place in the open spaces of Palestine, by the shores of a lake, up a mountain or on a level place. His great mentor John the Baptist drew people out of the Temple and out of the city down to the river to hear his message of renewal. Europe is full of great churches but they are empty and they are not what the Gospel is about. Stone is not tender. We are being called by this Pope to be disciples who follow Christ by finding and touching our neighbours with the love of God. It is not a new message, it is not a new revolution, but it has a new urgency.

Feed them yourselves

For those in the Catholic Church who encounter this message, it feels like a challenge. You can't just keep dawdling along as an "ordinary Catholic" who goes to Mass most weeks, believes most things the Church tells you and drops a few quid in the collection. I have felt this challenge acutely in recent years. To what extent are my lifestyle and my values indistinguishable from the good people in my neighbourhood who have no interest in God, Jesus, or the Church? I don't see a lot of difference; in fact in many ways they are more "Christian" than me with their commitment to the local community. We saw in Chapter 4 that the early Christians stood out because of how they lived. They were admired very often for their sincere commitment to the poor, for their kindness and compassion. I have been brought up since birth in the Catholic Church but only in recent years (at the time of writing I am fifty-two) do I feel really challenged or called to be a Christian disciple. My conscience has been well and truly bothered. What am I supposed to do? Sell my house and car and give the money to the poor? Isn't that what Jesus said in Luke's Gospel? I think my wife and children might have something to say about that. I think I just need to stay connected and like all Christians through the ages ask for the guidance of the Spirit about how to keep on growing in faith and understanding.

I have also asked myself what is my role in the Church. *Lumen Gentium* is very clear about the role of the laity in the modern world but what about the role of ordinary Catholics in the Church, especially a Church in the West which can rely less and less on the services of the clergy? The problem is we have a Church that has developed in recent years into a largely sacramental system which relied on priests for its operation and kept most of its members in a childlike state of observance. I recently attended a conference on this very problem and in one moment the answer was revealed to us. At the end of the day, four priests sat on the podium for the question-and-answer session. The youngest was around sixty and the eldest had a little nap during the discussion. One man stood up and with real passion and confusion in his voice said: "Fathers, today we have heard all the problems we face in the Church, now tell us what to do."

The tired faces of the clergy were enough of an answer to the question, but a woman stood up and provided the answer we needed to hear. "It has just struck me," she said, "that those who have been formed in the Church have a duty to form others. I'm reminded of that moment in the Gospels when the disciples panicked because of the number of people they had to feed and asked Jesus what they should do. Their instinct was to send them home. Jesus said: 'You give them something to eat.' [Luke 9:13] In other words, *feed them yourselves*. We can't keep looking to the clergy, or the bishop, or Rome for the answer. We need to get on and do this ourselves."

She received warm and sustained applause, having hit the proverbial nail on the head. I have since heard the phrase "feed them yourselves" breaking out in many other places as the Church seeks to come to terms with far fewer clergy. I have since asked myself how I intend to use my gifts in the little patch of English countryside that is my local Church. A central part of Sherry Weddell's programme for forming intentional Catholics is Called and Gifted workshops in which members of a parish are invited to discern their charisms and in what ways they might contribute fruitfully to the community (see "Resources for further study").

The intervention from the woman at the conference does raise another huge question which I do not have the competence to answer but must at least mention: the role of women in the Church. The comments from Mary John and Archie from the Philippines at the end of this chapter provide at least a glimpse of the frustration and at times anger at how women have been treated (and mistreated) in the Church. Francis has referred to the need for a "theology of women" which at least is a start. I'm not sure what he means by that and some of the women I have spoken to are not convinced either but it's probably better than nothing. It should also be noted, since we have spent a good deal of time looking at Vatican II, that few women were involved and no women addressed a Council session. In fact it was only when Cardinal Suenens remarked after the first two sessions that all of the lay observers were men that some women were invited to the third and fourth sessions. In Chapter 8 I attempt to offer a scriptural perspective on this question by looking briefly at the role of women in the community of the Beloved Disciple.

Fanning the flame

I'd like to finish this chapter with the recollection of an event which for me might sum up where the Church is headed in the next few years. With some students from my school I attended Flame 2 at the Wembley Arena in London, a huge gathering of young Catholics (and a few like me) organised by the Catholic Youth Ministry Federation in England and Wales. The event was addressed by Cardinal Louis Tagle of Manila and I sat there thinking: "Please God he will be the next Pope." He spoke just like Francis about the mercy of God with candour, humour and out of a deep personal sense of the healing presence of God. He is also from Asia and knows the problems faced by the poor, he knows the impact of climate change on ordinary people and he understands why globalisation is not always good news for local communities. If he's not the next Pope, then at least he will be one of the small group of men responsible for choosing him.

I was also very struck by the decision to hold Benediction towards the end of the event. The crowd at times were stirred up like a rock concert by the music and soaring atmosphere in the arena. Benediction, I thought, is not going to work. There is no way that eight thousand teenagers

136

will be able to calm down. How wrong I was. The Benediction in the Wembley Arena was similar in so many ways to the Sunday afternoon service I attended for years with my parents: the Blessed Sacrament in the golden monstrance, the Divine Praises (but modernised), and the waft of incense. What was so striking was the completely reverential response of the young audience and the palpable sense of God's presence which filled the huge auditorium. The Church of the present should always pass on what is best from the Church of the past.

There are some who are highly critical of such events in the Church. How many of those young people, they ask, will attend Mass regularly? Probably not many, and for very understandable reasons. The criticism is that such events provide a kind of spiritual high and discourage the kind of regular attendance the Church was founded upon. But that Church is changing, people are changing, and at least in that event the young people had a hugely positive experience of the Church and hopefully a personal encounter with their Lord and Saviour. What happens after that is up to us.

Gems from the Treasure Box #14

While the sacraments, particularly the Eucharist, remain essential to the Church's life, they are not the exclusive means of encounter with God's economy. This opens up the possibility of an enriched spirituality and allows people to understand the sacramental nature of their ordinary lives, hence the universal call to holiness. In a sense, every member of the Church – not just the ordained priesthood and hierarchy – becomes a minister of grace and has the possibility of mediating it in and through their lives.

Heythrop Institute for Religion, Ethics and Public Life, *On the Way to Life*

Comments from the twelve on the Church today and the role of the laity:

My remaining days are like a school for me. A school where you pass one test, you go to the next level. So I passed the test in choosing all of the material things, I passed that and I'm looking for other things. I passed the certain stages of being worthy. I'm finished with that, I'm finished chasing after material things. It's really like my soul trying to be more and more like Christ. I measure myself now to that kind of example, to the teachings of the Christ. However I can put it into practice, like this love for my fellow men and women (I'm gender sensitive now!), that is the only thing. It's really an overflowing love that you just want to put into practice. Sometimes it hurts you to see the suffering, to see all of the inequities in society, the injustices, it hurts you so much but it also pushes you to be vulnerable, to take risks, to stand up for the truth, for what is right, to always say the truth.

In fact as I've told them before, I'm not really the one that's protecting the truth, in reality it's the truth that's protecting me. If you're telling a lie, even with investigations and everything, pretty soon when you tell a lie you'll tell another lie and another lie and with all the interviews and investigations. I still have cases against me, I'm still being tried. If I was telling a lie somewhere in this past seven years I would have relented, forgotten some of those lies. So that's why I keep on insisting to people who tell me I'm the one protecting the truth, I say, "In reality it's the truth that's protecting me" and that faith in the truth has already taken over me.

Jun, 52, electronics engineer and whistle-blower

When Pope Francis came to visit the University of the Philippines he met the youth, so we were there with many of our students. We lined up and he came at 10am. The one who prepared the programme from the university and many of those who spoke were men, and so when they were saying their speeches we were all feeling uneasy and we were questioning why only men were giving speeches to the Pope. All of a sudden the Pope decided to let go of his planned speech and he said: "Where are the women? I only heard the voice of this little girl who could not even verbalise what she felt and all she did was to cry, because she was abused."

He was challenging the men because the men were really just talking about their accomplishments etc. and so he said: "The next time a Pope visits I hope there will be more women." We were clapping and cheering and saying: "Yes, yes, yes!" For me it was a very big leap in relation to women being recognised by the Church – the Catholic Church saying that women should have a voice – because for the longest time the voices of women have been suppressed by the Catholic Church and now the Pope is saying that we have to listen to the women because they have voices too, they have something to say which the men, according to Pope Francis, have not been listening to.

Mary John, 78, nun

In certain parishes here in this part of Manila, you can have women giving homilies, you can have women as altar servers but in other places it's a different thing altogether. No women can approach the altar. So the most that women can do during collection is the offertory; all the collections will just be at the steps, below the altar. They cannot bring it up to where the altar table is. It really depends on the bishop. But when you go out into the rural areas, especially the priests and the bishops who persevere in very difficult situations, that is where you see them very diligently working with people. They even get involved in some of the social issues, they participate in blocking trucks loaded with logs because of the anti-logging, so you have those types of bishops also.

Archie, 65, religious studies teacher

At fifty-six I've begun to recognise that institutions transmit cultures and, at one level, part of being a disciple is belonging to an institution as well as belonging to the body of Christ and it's very important to me to actually look after the institution so that the culture and the values can be transmitted. Catholic schools, for example, we get those because of an institutional Church that has to have resources, has to have a long-term plan. If you don't have Catholic schools the future of youth just simply dissolves because there's no formation and no education – hospitals, charities, all these elements – so I don't want to say that's the most important bit but I do actually want to say the institutional Church with its different organs is important.

How does one remain a disciple? I think at a personal level there is a very, very strong sense of seeking to learn how to love and to serve and to witness to truth. Interestingly I think Benedict was bringing this theme in near the end of his papacy: the role of the laity; what is it to be a Catholic lay person in a university; in a hospital; or unemployed; a mother. It's not just saying, "here are the correct doctrines," it's living a life which reflects something which is so special about Christ and in that sense I think discipleship is simply following Jesus in every moment of our lives.

Greg, 56, university teacher

And if you say that the most important thing about being Christian is to be baptised and to be engaged with the world to transform it for Christ then most of what the Church does is not what goes on inside the building that the priest does. One of the difficulties coming into Catholicism is this frustration with lay folk who think that it's not their job to do anything, either within the Church or within the world because it's up to the priests. I do find that frustrating, that's my biggest frustration. People say, "well I'll have to ask Father whether I can have Fairtrade coffee or not," and I think "just buy Fairtrade coffee!" That's what I find more frustrating, the fact that the laity seem to believe that they are children.

Wendy, 52, school teacher

We've got adults who've gone through their whole life and they're still praying for a new bike, if you know what I mean. Some priest recently was talking about confession and obviously without revealing sources and particular sins, he was saying: "I'm getting people coming to me who are much older and they're still confessing the same things they would have been confessing as a child, they haven't looked beyond that and there's no inner growth there and there's no spiritual maturity."

Paul, 23, chaplaincy assistant

I also think that if you've got faith and you've got that role as part of a congregation and a laity in a church, that's a vocation. Everyone's got a role to play in the Church – I think my role being in the Parish Council actually really helped me understand the importance of people in a church. A church isn't a church without its people so you don't necessarily have to have a career that's a vocation in order to feel like you're making a difference and being involved in something and creating something with your faith. It's hard because people think "I don't want to be a nun, I don't want to be a priest, I don't want to be a monk, therefore that's not a vocation" but actually just a calling to have faith does give you a sense of vocation – it definitely does for me anyway.

I don't really think you can live a life with other people, unless you're living a life completely isolated from anybody, without a sense of vocation. If you're a parent, that's vocation. Part of my wanting my little sister to grow up and do well, that's a sense of vocation. We've all got a sense of vocation. Not necessarily "I had this calling from God to go and be a teacher" but "my faith made me think that I should be the sort of person that would treat people well," and if you then go and treat people well then surely that's fulfilling a type of vocation.

Xita, 20, student

I think one of the big shifts in helping the Church recover that sense of the human vocation is in *Lumen Gentium* Chapter 5, the Universal Call to Holiness, because that is saying that there isn't this tiered system of religious life, priesthood, with a high road and then a low road for everybody else, marriage, the single life, whatever, being somehow a sort of second best, being immersed in the world and all the rest of it. I think that chapter in particular is one of the most revolutionary transformative chapters in *Lumen Gentium* because, although the language would be a little bit dated today, what it's actually saying is everyone has that vocation to holiness and that call to holiness. That then allows us to recover a genuine sense, a deep sense of the laity and the different forms, the way in which we live our Christian lives.

In fact that was always there because if you remember the old catechism: "Who made you? God made me. Why did God make me? To know, love and serve Him in this world and be happy with Him forever in the next." That's vocation, which means that everyone, just at a basic level of being human because everyone is created with that call to God because God creates each one of us uniquely for himself and so everyone, by virtue of their humanity, has a destiny, has a vocation to God and God's self. Then the deep question and the only really fundamental question of our lives is "how do I know him? How do I love him? How do I serve him in this life?" That then opens up the different way for each of us and that's why I think again along with that the Church can suddenly reappropriate the depth of married life, the depth of any life of service which is about knowing and loving and serving.

James, 64, religious order

Reflections for individuals

- In your journal write down your impressions of the Catholic Church today from your own point of view, either locally or nationally.

- What role, if any, do you see for yourself in the Church?

- Which of the comments from the twelve most strike a chord with you and why? What do the people around you think about the Church today?

Reflection activity for groups

- In your community consider the role of the clergy and the role of the laity – what more could the laity do to enrich and support the community? Consider drawing up an action plan to develop lay involvement with a small number of achievable targets to begin with.

Resources for further study

Sherry A. Weddell, *Forming Intentional Disciples* (Huntington: Our Sunday Visitor, 2012). The approach outlined in this book has been adopted as a programme by some dioceses as a way to introduce the era of the intentional disciple. There is not much mention of Vatican II and the theology of grace may seem somewhat old-fashioned (if correct) to some, but all the right questions are asked and there is a very helpful summary of the research on church attendance and patterns of belief.

Alan Schreck, *Rebuild my Church: God's Plan for Authentic Catholic Renewal* (Cincinnati: Servant Books, 2010). In this very scholarly but readable book, Alan Schreck provides a compelling history of renewal movements in the Church with the underlying thesis that renewal is not an issue for the hierarchy alone, but depends on every Catholic and their willingness to use their God-given gifts to help to discern and support renewal.

The Church in the Twenty-first Century, recorded talks by Fr Timothy Radcliffe OP, on https://www.youtube.com/watch?v=coynTl5oORQ, accessed 3 April 2015. In this series of ten-minute clips from a talk given in America in 2009, Fr Timothy, who is a most engaging speaker as well as a wonderful writer, explores how we can develop a confident Catholic culture in the years ahead which is open to the modern world without being completely assimilated.

Notes

[1] G. Vermes, *Christian Beginnings: From Nazareth to Nicea AD 30–325* (London: Penguin Books, 2012), 242

[2] Pew Research Center, *The Global Catholic Population*, http://www.pewforum.org/2013/02/13/the-global-catholic-population/, accessed 30 March 2015

[3] Pew Research Centre, *The Global Catholic Population*

[4] Timothy Radcliffe OP, *Take the Plunge: Living Baptism and Confirmation* (London: Bloomsbury, 2012), 261

[5] Sherry A. Weddell, *Forming Intentional Disciples* (Huntington: Our Sunday Visitor, 2012), 39

[6] Richard Rohr, *The Naked Now: Learning to See as the Mystics See* (New York: The Crossroads Publishing Company, 2009), 41

[7] Radcliffe, *Take the Plunge,* 191

[8] Radcliffe, *Take the Plunge,* 195

[9] Radcliffe, *Take the Plunge,* 199

[10] *Lineamenta* of the 2012 Synod Assembly, http://www.vatican.va/roman_curia/synod/documents/rc_synod_doc_20110202_lineamenta-xiii-assembly_en.html#_ftn36, accessed 2 April 2015

[11] Walter Kasper, *Pope Francis' Revolution of Tenderness and Love* (New Jersey: Paulist Press, 2015), 2

[12] Pope Francis, *Evangelii Gaudium* [The Joy of the Gospel], 3

[13] Daniel O'Leary, "One Dogmatic Certainty" in *The Tablet*, 21 March 2015

[14] http://w2.vatican.va/content/francesco/en/speeches/2014/december/documents/papa-francesco_20141222_curia-romana.html, accessed 10 January 2015

Chapter 6

Outside of ourselves – the search for holiness in the modern world

When I left the seminary at the age of nineteen I struggled to grow into an adult Christian. I had the support of my Catholic culture, my family, my seminary background, but that was not what was needed. When I went off to university, I phoned home every Sunday evening from a vandalised phone box (no mobile phones in those days) and faced the same litany of questions from my well-meaning father: yes, I had been to Mass (even if I hadn't); yes, I was saying my prayers (even if I wasn't); no, I was not all right for money. And that seemed to do the trick. That was Catholic enough, but in the meantime there was no growth, no transformation, no understanding of holiness beyond doing holy things, and not even doing them very well.

As we have heard from the twelve, many in the Church seem to be suffering from arrested development and do not understand how to mature in the faith. They are often brought up strongly in a Catholic culture, which includes a rich resource of prayers, devotions and sacramental practice (see James' and Tom's comments at the end of the chapter) but feel as if they are on their own when they try to grow beyond that stage. This is a problem when it comes to understanding what the Council fathers meant when they said that "all are called to holiness" (*LG*, 32). What is holiness for today's adult Catholic Christian?

There was much hope in the Church when the Rite of Christian Initiation of Adults (RCIA), based on the early

Church's way of initiating new members, was revived following the Council. In the past, adult converts were baptised following a course in catechetical instruction. It was more like an exam to be passed, as Evelyn Waugh so memorably satirised in *Brideshead Revisited* when the delightfully pragmatic and very wealthy American Rex Mottram needed to be "done" in order to gain the hand of the aristocratic Julia Flyte in marriage. RCIA was seen as the answer to the problem of adult formation, a genuine journey of faith leading to that credal proclamation we talked about in Chapter 4. We seemed to be breathing the same air as the early Church.

In *Forming Intentional Disciples*, one of the more disturbing revelations is the percentage of RCIA-prepared converts who leave the Church within the first year. Sherry Weddell reports a conversation with a senior churchman in Rome:

> We spent over an hour talking about our work with a particular cardinal in his office. At one point he turned to me and asked: "What percentage of American adults received through RCIA have left the practice of the faith within the first year?" I wasn't sure but knew the numbers weren't good so I hazarded a guess: "Fifty per cent?" The cardinal shook his head. "Oh no," he said, "it is closer to seventy per cent."[1]

Weddell's contention is that so many fall away because they are not sufficiently formed, or do not have enough support from intentional disciples to support them. The roots are too shallow. I sensed this phenomenon from my own parish experience but to hear it confirmed so bluntly in such a conversation must surely point to a fundamental problem. Why are people leaving the Church so soon after joining, and why are so many who have been members since childhood looking elsewhere for a more vibrant and engaging encounter with Jesus Christ? We have already established that the answer lies in the word "encounter". But why is it not part of the lived experience of many Catholics and what can we do to make it so? It now seems clear to me that you can go through all the Catholic motions and not have any sense of a personal encounter with God. So what can be done? As before, let us return to the source and consider the experience Jesus had of a personal encounter with God.

Gems from the Treasure Box #15

Late have I loved you, O Beauty ever ancient, ever new, late have I loved you! You were within me, but I was outside, and it was there that I searched for you. In my unloveliness I plunged into the lovely things which you created. You were with me, but I was not with you. Created things kept me from you; yet if they had not been in you they would not have been at all. You called, you shouted, and you broke through my deafness. You flashed, you shone, and you dispelled my blindness. You breathed your fragrance on me; I drew in breath and now I pant for you. I have tasted you, now I hunger and thirst for more. You touched me, and I burned for your peace.

St Augustine,
Confessions

He would withdraw to deserted places to pray

In all of the Gospels, but in Luke's in particular, Jesus is presented as one who prays. This in itself is no surprise since he came from a religious culture with a profound respect for its prayer tradition in the scriptures. He was familiar with the psalms, the prophets and of course the daily recital of the Shema. The Gospel writers all make the point that he often took himself off to "a lonely place", "to the other side", "alone", "up the mountain" and most strikingly in Luke when it says that he went to pray "as was his custom to the Mount of Olives" (Luke 22:39). Jesus prayed to his Father. It is this relationship which is one of the keys to his earthly ministry. He talked all the time about a kingdom yet he did not refer to God as a king but rather Father, or to use the transliterated Aramaic term *Abba*, which is an endearment meaning something like "daddy, papa". His mission, his understanding of God and who he was, was funded by this intimate, mystical union. This is what makes the abandonment on the cross in Mark's Gospel all the more heartbreaking. In his desperate cry of anguish, Jesus uses the more abstract *Eloi*, meaning God.

The most dramatic event in the prayer life of Jesus was perhaps the transfiguration, which is recorded in all three synoptic Gospels with a different emphasis in each, but in Luke's Gospel it is very much a prayer event. Jesus takes his inner circle – Peter, James and John – up on the mountain "to pray" (Luke 9:28). It was while he was praying that "the appearance of his face changed" (Luke 9:29) and his clothes become dazzling. As always with Luke, the disciples are not portrayed as entirely useless.

They were tired but managed to stay awake, although they do display the classic Catholic tendency in the face of mystery: "Let us make three dwellings" (Luke 9:33). The clue to the meaning of this event is provided by the voice from the cloud, "This is my Son, my Chosen; listen to him" (Luke 9:35). Denis McBride, in his reading of this passage, makes the point that if this was the Father's answer to the prayer of Jesus, then what was the question?

The implication is that Jesus was prayerfully searching for his identity and purpose and he is made radiant by the answer. McBride comments that: "No one can hold securely on to his or her identity without the support of significant others."[2] Jesus has been named in love by the Father and that is what gives him the sense of driven purpose to continue his mission, to set his face towards Jerusalem. The transfiguration of Jesus in Luke is not so much the triumphalist display we find depicted by Titian and other Renaissance artists; it is a mystical prayer experience of communion with God. McBride comments further that transfiguration happens over and over again in the Gospel: "Throughout his public ministry, Jesus transfigures many people – the broken, the wounded, the wayward. He calls to the deepest part of people; he sees in the afflicted more than others see."[3]

The first thing Jesus does when he comes down from the mountain is to heal the boy who is seized by a demon. He is an only son and his distraught father turns to Jesus for help: "Teacher, I beg you to look at my son…" (Luke 9:38). Jesus is cross that his disciples couldn't do much with the boy, but heals him anyway. Jesus, the transfigured Son, who has been newly affirmed in the love of his Father, heals the son who is disfigured by possession, as so many of us are, one way or another. Literature tells that story over and over: who is broken and who is restored by love in the human comedy? Philip Larkin, in the poem "Faith Healing", memorably presents the lost and the least, the quirky and the cracked (finely balancing contempt and compassion), filing up to the American faith healer, since nowhere else in their lives could they come close to that kind of loving attention.

Just as what disfigures people is the absence of love, so what transfigures or transforms them is the presence of love, or being named and called in love. The divine presence that transfigured Jesus is the same presence that works through him in others. It is also the same presence that is available to us in prayer. If we are open to the divine life, we will be on a journey towards transformation and will be more able to face whatever is put in front of us, as Jesus was. It seems to me that this is the key to growth in holiness. Not so much a lifetime of observance or getting it right but, after the example of Jesus, a routine commitment to deep prayer in the confidence that *Abba*, the divine presence with the loving gaze of a parent, will name us and allow us to become "sharers in the divine nature" (*LG*, 40). Getting it right, or *attentiveness*, will naturally follow.

Saint John Paul II, whose phenomenal output we seem to be just coming to terms with, published *Novo Millennio Ineunte* ("At the Beginning of the New Millennium"; *NMI*)] to mark the end of the Jubilee Year 2000. In that apostolic letter he addresses the question of how we can come

Gems from the Treasure Box #16

In everyone there sleeps A sense of life lived according to love. To some it means the difference they could make By loving others, but across most it sweeps As all they might have done had they been loved.

Philip Larkin,
"Faith Healing"

to faith. How did Peter come to faith from his initial declaration of unworthiness? (Luke 5:8). He turns to Luke's Gospel and the example of Jesus "praying alone" (Luke 9:18) and then provides for the faithful a very clear and practical directive for the life of faith:

> We cannot come to fullness of contemplation of the Lord's face by our own efforts alone, but by allowing grace to take us by the hand. Only *the experience of silence and prayer* offers the proper setting for the growth and development of a true, faithful and consistent knowledge of that mystery.[4]

The emphasis in the text is John Paul II's, not mine, showing how emphatically he believed in the importance of this point for the followers of Christ at the beginning of the third millennium. Our request then becomes the same as the disciples': "Lord, teach us how to pray" (Luke 11:1). The disciples asked this question because they must have felt, as we do, that their traditional prayer resources were no longer a match for their new sense of discipleship. Throughout the Gospels there are recollections of the many ways Jesus responded to that request, either directly or in parables.

In Luke's Gospel, for example, we find the parable of the Pharisee and the Tax Collector (Luke 18:9-14). They both go to the Temple to pray, but one gets it wrong and the other gets it right, according to Jesus. The Pharisee thinks he gets it all right, he does it by the book, in fact he does more than he should in terms of observance. There is no suggestion that he is a bad man, and yet it is the tax collector, the sinner, whom Jesus says is at rights with God. Why? Although the Pharisee thinks he is in God's favour because of what he does, he trusts in himself and "regarded others with contempt" (Luke 18:9). He has no ministry for those who are by law seen as wicked people: the thieves, rogues, adulterers, tax collectors; the very ones Jesus has come to save. He is full of his own sense of accomplishment, whereas the tax collector is full of his need for God: "Be merciful to me, a sinner!" (18:13). The tax collector, in the words of Saint John Paul II, has allowed grace to take him by the hand.

In the kingdom of God presented to us by Jesus, there is no room for contempt of others and there is no spiritual growth for those who trust in themselves. Jesus is saying that you need a spirit of humble surrender to God, knowing that you cannot bring anything to the altar but your own inadequacy. Then there is room for God. The point is reinforced in the next passage in Luke's Gospel when Jesus blesses the little children and says that the kingdom of God belongs to these, the powerless ones. In Matthew's Gospel there is more advice about the state one should be in when one prays. For Jesus so much depends on the condition of your heart. He says if you are angry or unreconciled with your brothers or sisters: "Leave your gift before the altar and go; first be reconciled" (Matthew 5:24). The God of Jesus is really not interested in show or perfect performances, but rather a humble heart which is ready to forgive and be forgiven.

Jesus offers some very practical advice in Matthew's Gospel. He is speaking again of the dangers of showboating, of using public prayer as a means of displaying our own worthiness. Jesus is certainly not speaking against community prayer as such: "For where two or three are gathered in my name, I am there among them" (Matthew 18:20). And as we have said from the beginning, being a Catholic Christian is fundamentally *ecclesial*, it means being part of a Church. However, the message seems to be that praying in common is not enough and can become *merely* a community event. We have seen that Jesus often withdrew to pray on his own. This is what deepened his relationship with the Father and his understanding of his own identity and mission. It is consistent with his own practice, therefore, when he says: "Whenever you pray, go into your room and shut the door and pray to your Father who is in secret" (6:6). And when you're there, don't "heap up empty phrases" (Matthew 6:7). I don't think there's any way round this one: silence and solitude seem to be important.

Gems from the Treasure Box #17

The religious interest of the prisoners, as far and as soon as it developed, was the most sincere imaginable. The depth and vigor of religious belief often surprised and moved a new arrival. Most impressive in this connection were the improvised prayers or services in the corner of a hut, or in the darkness of the locked cattle truck in which we were brought from a distant work site, tired, hungry and frozen in our ragged clothing

Viktor E. Frankl,
Man's Search for Meaning

Shallow prayer

In the recent history of the Church we have frowned somewhat on contemplative practice, seeing it as something reserved for the monks and the mystics. It had been a central part of Christianity for hundreds of years but was largely lost in the post-Tridentine focus on sacraments and structures. Following the encouragement of Saint John Paul II, many in the Church, not just Karl Rahner (see *Gems* #11) now regard the practice of contemplation, or some form of personal prayer life, as the key to the formation of disciples. It is in deep prayer that we experience the loving presence of God, the "encounter" that so many are searching for, that we actually begin to change.

The problem is that so many of us do not know how to pray as adults and, I suspect, that most of us have forgotten the sound of silence. The first problem is a result of our upbringing. As we can see from the comments of the twelve, those who were brought up in the Catholic faith were taught many prayers and devotions. And rightly so. This is important for young people because it gives them the language of the divine which they will no longer hear in our society: *holy, adore, grace.* I remember a talk from one priest on the importance of Catholic education. He said that every day in his diocese, 20,000 young people heard the name of Jesus spoken in reverence. It also gives them an early sense, as Rebecca says in Chapter 1, that there is a God, an abiding presence. However, this childhood prayer is often a simplistic form of petition, asking for things. Many of us do not grow out of that (see Xita, Wendy and Paul's comments at the end of the chapter).

This was certainly my experience. Over the years, when I was feeling more drawn to the spiritual life I reached for my traditional prayers (like saying the rosary on long commutes to work) but those practices soon fell away. I had no understanding of what I was doing and why. What was supposed to be happening? Why could I not feel anything? If prayer is about asking for things then is it only those who pray well who manage to convince God to respond? John Paul II calls this "shallow prayer" (*NMI*, 34) and is very clear that it is not enough for Christians. In fact, in the face of the trials facing us today, he proposes that this type of prayer would place us "at risk" of mediocrity (*NMI*, 34). The prophets of the modern age are trying to help us to grow up. Enzo Bianchi, the prior of an ecumenical monastic community in Italy, puts it this way:

> The aim of prayer, in fact, is to attain that point where we do the will of God, not that God should do our will. Our prayers do not change the plan of God's love for us, but it is the gifts which God grants in prayer which transform us and which bring us into harmony with his will.[5]

When I read that I thought: *"That's it, in a nutshell, finally!"* Richard Rohr is fond of saying in his talks that the answer to every prayer to God... is God. What we receive or "find" (Luke 11:9) is more of a share in the divine nature. If we commit to this journey in the spirit of the tax collector or a child then we will change slowly but surely or, as Saint Paul says, we will be "transformed into the same image from one degree of glory to another" (2 Corinthians 3:18). This does not mean that we should not pray for others, but it means that we should not seek to bargain with God or persuade him to make our sick friend better. In "The Joy of the Gospel", Pope Francis reminds us that Saint. Paul's prayers were full of people and that authentic contemplation always has a place for others. But when it comes to intercession he says basically the same thing as Bianchi and Rohr; in other words that God "is always there first"(*EG*).[6] However, the transforming effect of prayer is that "when evangelizers rise from prayer, their hearts are more open; freed from self-absorption, they are desirous of doing good and sharing their lives with others" (*EG*, 282). We are more attentive because of prayer to the needs of our sick friend; how God chooses to order the destiny of individuals is a mystery beyond our reckoning.

True joy on earth

The transformation of the individual as the central movement of the spiritual journey is a concept that has been rediscovered by the modern contemplative movement. Thomas Merton, an American Trappist monk, was one of its most influential advocates in the twentieth century. His fundamental point is that the journey of transformation is from the False Self to the True Self. The False Self is not bad, it is just limited. Richard Rohr maintains that the False Self is what gives us the juice for the first half of life. It is like our "default" setting, with whatever drives, motivations, qualities and habits we were born with and formed with. Grace is at work there too, of course, but in its unreconstructed state it is basically our ego in charge of our progress through life. The True Self is the aim of all contemplative practice, one might say the aim of the Christian life:

> The only true joy on earth is to escape from the
> prison of our own false self and enter by love
> into union with the life who dwells and sings
> within the essence of every creature and in the
> core of our souls.[7]

Merton is adamant that the prison of our own false self
is not the body. For him, like Jesus, like Saint Paul, the
body is a temple of God and should not be desecrated.
The "marriage" of body and soul in one person is one of
the things which make us the image of God. For too long
in the Christian tradition we assumed that if we were
to be transformed into the divine image then it was the
body that had to be denied or suffer, since the body was
corrupt, fallen and prone to sin. We should have looked
more closely at the life of Jesus. While John the Baptist
pursued the ascetical path, with rough clothes and rough
food, Jesus showed no inclination to follow the same path
as his mentor. He was often accused of being something
of a glutton and a drunk (Luke 7:34). The contemplative
movement gives us a new and compelling way to
understand the wisdom of Jesus. When he says you must
deny yourself and take up your cross, the self which must
be denied is not the poor old body which gets old and
dies but the False Self, which is also passing.

This is a major insight and liberation for people of the
modern age. The False Self, or the ego as Freud called
it, is a fragile creation. We not only have to deal with
the adult motivations arising from childhood traumas,
but we have to cope with the pressures of negotiating
the pace and priorities of a modern society which
values performance, success and status above all. We
are constantly being measured and evaluated: in work,

in public, in private, online. What we drive, where we live, what we wear, how we speak, have become the "shibboleths" of our standing in society. What is worse is that we have internalised this process and evaluate ourselves, constantly taking the temperature of the private/ false self – *how am I doing, how do I feel, what do I need?* The irony is that the modern age has rediscovered the mortification of the flesh, hence the trend for fasting or detoxing, but the aim of such practice is only to make the body look and perform better. It still keeps us outside of ourselves when the truth, the secret, the treasure, is within.

Gems from the Treasure Box #18

If I had a message to my contemporaries it is surely this: Be anything you like, be madmen, drunks and bastards of every shape and form, but at all costs avoid one thing: success. If you are too obsessed with success, you will forget to live. If you have learned only how to be a success, your life has probably been wasted.

Thomas Merton,
Love and Living

Jesus describes the kingdom of God as being like a treasure "hidden in a field" (Matthew 13:44) and the person who discovers this treasure goes and sells everything to purchase the field. Nothing else matters. In another use of the field image, Jesus illustrates just how you know what matters to you. He says that: "Where your treasure is, there your heart will be also" (Luke 12:34). That saying is often carelessly rendered as where your heart is there will your treasure be, but that's not what it says. Jesus is saying show me your *treasure* and I'll tell you what's in your heart. That stunning saying comes at the end of one of Luke's most beautiful passages when Jesus, speaking so strongly to the stressed and anxious people of the modern age, says: "Do not worry about your life" (Luke 12:22). So many of us, Christians included, have only junk in our treasure boxes: our status at work, the size of our waistline, our need to be popular. Whatever is in our treasure box is what educates our heart. Luke says forget that, look for a treasure that will last, and you don't have to look very far.

It took me a very long time to take seriously a great truth that I had heard over the years: God is within you. In the pre-Vatican II Church God was *extra*, outside of us, ensconced in heaven. Our purpose was to attain the reward of joining him but so often we experienced failure because God seemed so perfect, so remote. When one begins to take an interest in the Gospels and the history

> ## Gems from the Treasure Box #19
>
> We have this treasure in clay jars, so that it may be made clear that this extraordinary power belongs to God and does not come from us. We are afflicted in every way, but not crushed; perplexed, but not driven to despair; persecuted, but not forsaken; struck down, but not destroyed.
>
> St Paul,
> Second Letter to the
> Corinthians

of Christian thought, that is not the message we hear. In Gems #15 we read the famous prayer of Saint Augustine who realised late in life that God was within. Saint Paul makes the same point in many places, including his letter to the Romans: "The Spirit of God dwells in you" (Romans 8:9). The saints and mystics lived with this perception as part of their daily reality. It was all too much for Saint Catherine of Genoa, who ran through the streets shouting, "my deepest me is God". In the Orthodox tradition it is called *theosis* or "divinisation" which begins in this life and is completed in heaven. The second letter of St Peter, using the phrase which we have already seen in *Lumen Gentium*, says that we can "become participants of the divine nature" (2 Peter 1:4). It makes sense when you think about it: where else would we experience God? But the question remains, how do we find this treasure that is "not far from each one of us"? (Acts 17:27).

On Mount Horeb, Elijah did not find God in the earthquake or the fire, but surprisingly he finally met God in "sheer silence" (1 Kings 19:12). It is interesting to note that the King James Bible translation uses the phrase "still small voice" which many of us are familiar with, but the New Revised Standard Version (Catholic Edition), which is a more literal translation, uses "sheer silence". There is quite a difference between a voice, no matter how small, and silence. In the contemplative tradition, silence is very important, or in the words of Thomas Keating: "God's first language is silence."[8] We have known for a very long time how to meet our God but we just seem to have let it slip our minds. For those who want to discover how to practise this contemplative meeting of God in silence there needs to be some guidance. If you want to start a fitness regime, you don't just buy the first pair of trainers you come across and disappear over the hill. You may never be seen again. You could, at least, purchase *Running Monthly* and research the best trainers and the best diet. There is no one way to approach contemplative prayer but one technique that's widely followed, developed by Trappist monks in America in the 1970s, is Centering Prayer (I'll keep the American spelling!).

I have only just begun to try and practise this type of prayer so I have little to offer by way of advice or guidance but I will say that it feels like a proper work of the spirit, an *ascesis*. Thomas Keating recommends two twenty-minute sessions of silence each day. For some that will be difficult enough. It is only because our children are older now that I have any chance of two minutes of silence, let alone twenty. It might require setting the alarm a bit earlier. The format is so simple:

after an invocation to the Holy Spirit (*epiclesis*) you are invited to let go of your thoughts (which are mostly the habitual and obsessive scripts of the False Self) and consent to the active presence of God in us, to "deepen our contact with the Divine Indwelling".[9] A simple "sacred word" (but not a mantra) is used to bring you back to silence when the thoughts crowd in, which they will, but less so with practice.

Keating is adamant that "if people are never exposed to some kind of non-conceptual prayer, it may never develop at all because of the overly intellectual bias of Western culture".[10] Forget about the tyranny of relativism, Keating is concerned about the *tyranny of thinking*, closely followed by the tyranny of noise, increasingly digital noise. Of course God can get through any obstacle but we make it harder for him by maintaining this constant wall of thinking and over-stimulation between us and the peace of the divine, "which surpasses all understanding" (Philippians 4:7). This is not, by the way, some monastic retreat from the world, or from thinking. As we will see in the next chapter, the true contemplative always comes back to the world after the refreshment of deep prayer with greater attentiveness and more fruitful thoughts.

> **Gems from the Treasure Box #20**
>
> Anyone who does not win feels that he is no good in this culture, whereas in the quiet of deep prayer, you are a new person, or rather, you are you.
>
> Thomas Keating,
> *Open Mind, Open Heart*

Lectio Divina

There are other great prayer traditions in the Church, often inspired by one of the saints and promoted by one of the religious orders. The Jesuits, for example, have an approach to prayer based on the *Spiritual Exercises* of Saint Ignatius of Loyola – see *God of Surprises* by Gerard W. Hughes (London: Darton, Longman & Todd, 2008). Another tradition which I have some experience of and which Saint John Paul II explicitly recommends in *Novo Millennio Ineunte* is *Lectio Divina*, or the prayerful reading of the scriptures. *Lectio* goes back to the beginnings of the monastic movement and was very common in the Church for many hundreds of years, especially in Benedictine communities. There is now a significant revival of this practice.

There are four classic stages for the individual or group beginning with *lectio,* the careful reading of the scripture passage (perhaps the readings of the day, or for the forthcoming Sunday). This first stage is worth some emphasis. In my day job I read a lot. I read quickly with the purpose of extracting information. The attention span of modern men and women is short and jagged (I heard recently that we were down to eight seconds, which is a concern). We are forgetting how to read well and with attention. Enzo Bianchi recommends even writing out the scripture passage in long hand as a way of really absorbing it into our mind and spirit. Up until as late as the medieval period people only read aloud; there was no "private" or interior reading. Perhaps we could try that, as long as we warn anybody we live with first. Whatever technique is used, the *lectio* stage should not be taken for granted. Take your time, take God's time.

The next traditional stage is *meditatio,* the exploration of the deeper meaning of the text. I have attended workshops on *Lectio Divina* with Benedictine monks and they shared with us a method for group *lectio* which invited "echoes", or the sharing of insights on the reading by the group. It is very powerful and can be very moving. It is important to remember that the echoes are first-person comments on what the reading says to me; they should not prompt discussion. Then *oratio,* the prayers arising from the meditation, and finally *contemplatio,* perhaps more suited to personal *lectio* when a period of sustained silence brings us to God's presence in us and the joy of that indwelling. For those who may feel anxious about starting with Centering Prayer, *lectio* may be more suitable. It really depends on where you are in the journey, your temperament and your lifestyle.

It is so important to stress that there are many ways to pray. I have tried to convey something of my own struggle to come to the point in my life where I believe that prayer is of vital importance to my Christian discipleship. In my current circumstances, Centering Prayer seems to be answering a deep need for a silent encounter with the loving and life-giving reality of God. I do not intend in any way to demean or dismiss the popular devotions of the Church, many of which I have fond memories of from my Catholic upbringing. When I was in Manila I saw the Black Nazarene being carried through the choked and chaotic streets, I saw students kiss the statue of Our Lady of Montserrat before exams and a community stop in its tracks to say the Angelus at midday. All these beloved traditions, although they can lead to superstition and complacency, are also powerful "signs" of God's presence in a world with more need of it than ever.

In my own attempts to deepen my experience of prayer I have learned some important points. It seems to be absolutely fundamental that you persevere and make time for daily prayer, whatever form it takes. All the writers, prophets and spiritual masters say this and Jesus himself is our role model. It is a discipline, a work of the spirit, and should not be undertaken just when you feel like it. Enzo Bianchi puts it very strongly when he says that: "Anyone who claims not to have time for prayer in reality is confessing to idolatry."[11] At first I was affronted by that comment and thought: "*Enzo, have you any idea of how busy I am and how stressful my life is?*" Once I had got over myself I knew of course that he was absolutely correct. His point is that if we claim to be Christians and say we don't have time for prayer then everything else that consumes our time is more important. That's idolatry. He insists that Christians must resist the "ideology of work and of alienating productivity".[12] It is a tough challenge but it cuts right to the heart of the dilemma facing many who call themselves Christian today. "You cannot serve God and wealth" (Luke 16:13).

Finally, our prayers must bear fruit. If we pray like the Pharisee, getting it all right but still clinging to a rotten treasure in our heart, then we will be what Saint Paul calls a "noisy gong, or a clanging cymbal" (1 Corinthians 13:1). If we are in the process of being gradually transformed by the deepening presence of God within us then it will be evident. In the words of Thomas Keating we will "gain a spirit of thanksgiving and compassion, discernment, patience and peace".[13] If we are truly bearing fruit in our discipleship then it will result in a new way of looking on reality and behaving towards others, beginning with our nearest and dearest. We will be more alive, spiritually attentive and joyful. When we are becoming free in God it is only the beginning of the great journey, there is still much to do: "I am sure God doesn't intend merely to look at these people who are so holy. He wants them to do something. If he liberates them from their false selves, it is precisely for some great purpose." 14 This is the other dimension of holiness which we will look at next, the doing part.

Gems from the Treasure Box #21

We really live outside of ourselves. There are very few humans who truly live inside themselves and this is why there are so many problems... In each person's heart, there is something like a small, intimate space, where God comes down to speak alone with that person. And this is where a person determines his or her own destiny, his or her own role in the world. If each of the people with so many problems were to enter at this moment this small space, and, once there, were to listen to the voice of the Lord which speaks in our own conscience, how much could each one of us do to improve the environment, society, the family with whom we live?

Blessed Oscar Romero,
Through the Year with Oscar Romero: Daily Meditations

Comments from the twelve on the search for holiness

Do I believe that when I pray I will get things? I don't know, that seems kind of a cheating "I'll pray for that and then it will happen" but I think when you pray for something or better than that someone, it gives you that positive attitude. I think prayer brings positivity and that's what's really important to me. But it's about it being personal and about it being "I don't want to shout about it. I don't want to tell people that I'm praying." It's a time to be quiet in a world where everything else is just so loud, for me. It's become really important in being grateful for what I've got. I think there are not that many opportunities now in life to be grateful for the things that are good but prayer does give you that.

Xita, 20, student

I heard a Franciscan talking recently about prayer and he said something along the lines of, you probably shouldn't quote this: "If your prayer life is only Mass on a Sunday, that's like a married couple making love but never talking", something like that. It was this idea that there's more to a marriage than just that, you've got to talk and you've got to love each other and be there for each other. It goes back to what I was saying previously, death by sacrament. There's a lot more to the spiritual life than that. A lot of priests I know spend an hour, half an hour, before the Blessed Sacrament every day. They'll say Mass but it's only a part of what they do. There needs to be this inner personal relationship and a real need for salvation and to pray regularly. In an ideal world everyone would have a spiritual director. We have psychologists, doctors, you go to the gym, you've got your personal trainer, I just think prayer is a big part of that. I think you need someone you can bounce ideas off. It doesn't mean you need to see them every week but I just think it's something that in an ideal world everyone would have.

Paul, 23, chaplaincy assistant

I've always been uncomfortable with the bidding prayers at Mass because I think: "Well, we asked God for that last week and he's obviously not listening so why are we saying it again for world peace and all that?" So whenever I've written prayers I've tried not to ask God for anything. The Divine Office has prayers that basically say "may we do something". So on Mondays it's about strengthening the people who feed the hungry, give courage to those who give drink to the thirsty, and I find that a challenge because I'm praying this prayer about: "Dear God, help people to do this" and I go: "Well, but what about you, Wendy, what are you actually going to do about this?" So yes, I think you're right that intercession ought to change us; we should be the answer to our own prayer. I think the kind of prayer that says: "I really don't know what to do about this" is a great prayer. The kind of prayer that says: "God, you do something about it" is not such a great prayer.

Wendy, 52, school teacher

I remember reading criticism of the way people behaved in church about the time of the Council and some people would read the Missals and other people would say the rosary and I was a man who just said a lot of Hail Marys. I think I know more now about why I say a lot of Hail Marys but I don't really go beyond the basic Lord's Prayer and invocation of the Holy Spirit and rosary sometimes. I get a lot out of the psalms but that's perhaps because I'm in the choir and have to know what I'm saying and that certainly is a difference. But no, I think I was very much a child of the times. I say my prayers

168

but I always remember saying to my father once before Saturday morning confession: "I haven't got very much to confess except I didn't say my prayers a couple of times", and he said: "Not saying prayers is not a sin, it is an imperfection."

Tom, 78, retired schoolmaster

What I introduced to them are some antiphons from the psalms so for five years now I have introduced them to Psalm 46, the antiphon, *Be still and know that I am God*. We start with "be", just the word "be" and we comment about it and then the next phrase would be "be still" and then "be still and know", so what do you know in stillness, and then "be still and know that I am", what is this I am? So they have to be real. And then "be still and know that I am God". So at the end of it all I say "Be and God are related because God's name is…" and then I tell the girls, because it is all women, how stillness is very important for women as a moment to pause but also as a moment to be aware. Especially awareness of danger, awareness of attack, threat, so that they will know what to do because sometimes violence happens because they're unaware that it's about to happen because they don't pay attention.

There was one student who was my student in two gender courses, Women's Studies and Gender and Media, and she says: "I still carry the prayer, that's what I learned from you, 'Be still and know.'" What stayed with her is be still and know that I am God. That's good enough. The theories, she can look up, but the appreciation of being able to pray and that's the antiphon that she remembers, well, fine with me. Sometimes I light a candle. Once the light is out, that's the end of the prayer.

Archie, 65, religious studies teacher

I have slowly learnt how to pray, partly through being in therapy for a period which was hugely helpful because I think it allowed me to recognise that I didn't have to fill up all the space and that prayer could involve a silence which would also, not only allow me to hear God but it would allow me to hear parts of self which need healing or can pray more than my will. There's that statement by John Paul II that every true prayer comes from the Holy Spirit and I think there's something really profound there.

Basically my day starts with prayer when I walk the dog, so I'm a very antisocial dog walker, I avoid people and walk the park with my rosary in my pocket and try and mix my prayer-life between spontaneous and structured prayer. I say that because sometimes the structure holds me to just keep my attention but the structured prayer for me would be deadening if it was the only type of prayer, so I often do just start the day with a kind of "being honest to God" session. Simply saying "I'm totally exhausted, I don't want to go and do any of what I've got to do" and try and bring myself into the presence of God, usually through just trying to be honest with myself. I think that's, for me, been the kind of very important way of almost like an examination of conscience because it allows me to recognise again my immense selfishness, it knows no bounds.

Greg, 56, university teacher

The Carthusians have that great tradition of prayer through the small hours of the morning and while I was praying in their community I had a great sense that the prayer that was being offered was not just for us in this monastery but for those who were struggling at that time, those small desperate hours of the morning, those who were on the streets, those who were dying, those who were in some difficulty, so in this wonderful, beautiful deep paradoxical way, although you were in the enclosed life, you were absolutely open to the world and to its needs. That sense has never left me; that there's always this great community of prayer that's operating and you don't need to know that it's there in that sense but it supports us.

Contemporary existence at so many levels, whether it's the anxiety about the economy or how to bring up the family or how just to live with all the increasing demands upon us, leaves us rather bruised and battered and we need a place of peace. I think Pope Francis has it absolutely right when he talks about the Church being a field hospital, but that's a field hospital that begins with prayer, that's why I think there is this wonderful rediscovery of Adoration. I do think that the Blessed Sacrament is profoundly healing; I think it heals also because it creates that space, that peaceful space in which we can rest, it's like the deer that longs for running streams, it's like being led beside those waters and those green pastures. It's God himself who nourishes us, that deeper search in some way to come to the source of life. We as a Church have that, we have that richness, and particularly as a Catholic Church we have these wonderful spiritual traditions from the founders of religious orders and others. That's an extraordinary outpouring of the Spirit.

James, 64, religious order

Reflections for individuals

- What has been your own experience of prayer and growth in holiness? Who do you pray to, how do you pray? Has your attitude to prayer been changed or challenged in any way having read this chapter?

- What strikes you about Jesus' approach to prayer? Did anything surprise you about the advice he gave to his disciples?

- Which of the Gems or which comments from the twelve on the subject of holiness/ prayer strike a chord with you in particular? Why do you think that is?

Reflection activity for groups

- What is the prayer life or prayer routine of your group or community? How do you support members of the group to grow in their adult Christian faith?

Resources to support further study and reflection on the search for holiness

Enzo Bianchi, *Why Pray, How to Pray* (London: St Paul's, 2014). This is an excellent introduction to the topic of prayer. The approach of Enzo Bianchi is steeped in scripture as well as the tradition of the Church. For those who wish to find out more about the theology and tradition of the different types of prayer – petition, intercession, praise, thanksgiving, blessing – I would recommend starting here.

Enzo Bianchi, *Lectio Divina: From God's Word to Our Lives* (London: SPCK, 2015). For those who feel drawn to *Lectio Divina* as the most appropriate way to develop their spiritual lives, there is no better place to start than this book. Bianchi provides an illuminating history of scripture in the Church as well as explaining the importance of *Lectio* itself.

Thomas Keating, *Open Mind, Open Heart* (London: Continuum, 2006). This is the first in a trilogy by the Cistercian (Trappist) monk which also includes *Imitation to Love* and *The Mystery of Christ*. For those who feel drawn to centering prayer as the most appropriate way to develop their spiritual lives, this is the place to start. The book includes genuine frequently asked questions from ordinary people who have tried to develop this technique in their own lives.

Richard Rohr, *The Naked Now* (New York: The Crossroad Publishing Company, 2009). If you feel drawn to the style of Rohr, as I do, then he will cover just about everything in his inspirational flow of publications and talks. In this book he provides an accessible and scripture-based account of the importance of the contemplative tradition and many practical examples for the contemplatives of today. It is sometimes better just to stay with one author for a while and access the wisdom of the tradition through them.

Christopher Jamison OSB, *Finding Happiness* (London: Weidenfeld & Nicolson, 2008). There was a very successful TV series a few years ago called *The Monastery*, when the possibility of the contemplative life for ordinary people was presented to the national consciousness in a very interesting and engaging way by Fr Christopher Jamison. In this book of the series, Fr Christopher takes us into the wisdom of the Benedictine tradition and helps us to deal with our thoughts, which are often the root of our problems.

https://sacredspace.ie. This popular daily prayer website has been run by the Irish Jesuits since 1999 and has received many millions of hits over the years. I know several people who find it an ideal way to fit in some reflective prayer during a busy schedule. Inspired by the spirituality of the founder of the Jesuits, Saint Ignatius of Loyola, the format is the same each day: Presence of God, Freedom, Consciousness, The Word, Conversation, Conclusion.

Notes

[1] Sherry Weddell, *Forming Intentional Disciples* (Huntington: Our Sunday Visitor, 2012), 170

[2] Denis McBride C.Ss.R., *Jesus and the Gospels* (Chawton: Redemptorist Publications, 2002),134

[3] McBride, *Jesus and the Gospels*, 135

[4] Saint John Paul II, *Novo Millennio Ineunte*, http://w2.vatican.va/content/john-paul-ii/en/apost_letters/2001/documents/hf_jp-ii_apl_20010106_novo-millennio-ineunte.html, 31, accessed 9 April 2015

[5] Enzo Bianchi, *Why Pray How to Pray* (London: St Paul's Publishing, 2014), 49

[6] Pope Francis, *Evangelii Gaudium*, 283

[7] Thomas Merton, *New Seeds of Contemplation* (New York: New Directions, 1972), 25

[8] Thomas Keating, *Open Mind, Open Heart* (London, Bloomsbury, 2006), 48

[9] Keating, *Open Mind*, 35

[10] Keating, *Open Mind*, 154

[11] Enzo Bianchi, *Why Pray, How to Pray* (London: St Paul's Publishing, 2014), 85

[12] Bianchi, *Why Pray*, 85

[13] Keating, *Open Mind*, 84

[14] Keating, *Open Mind*, 111

Global and grounded – the Catholic Church and the common good

Holiness is not a private matter. The impression I often had growing up in my Catholic culture in Scotland was that holiness was some kind of private negotiation between the soul and God with the aim of achieving the reward of eternal life. There also seemed to be a divide between what happened in church and the rest of your life, and going to church didn't seem to make much difference to the way people lived. We seemed to be the same as everybody else. As we saw in Chapter 1, you could tell the Catholics because of their Irish surnames and which football team they supported on a Saturday, but you wouldn't say that you could tell they were Christians by their love (John 13:35). That is not to say that there were not many loving Catholics, but the primary identity was tribal. Catholics did not stand out in society like the early Christians because they behaved radically differently. They may have had different beliefs and customs but in a crowded high street you would have struggled to set them apart.

The pre-Vatican II focus on the soul's journey to heaven meant that there was not a great focus on love of neighbour in the here and now. That was mostly left to the religious orders. There were some lay organisations with a charism for the alleviation of poverty. My father was a great supporter of the Saint Vincent de Paul Society, which raised money from the occasional second collection at Mass to help people in the parish who were poor. For the most part, we did not have a language for social action and only the beginnings of an understanding of the global dimension of poverty and injustice. In our parish we did have the legendary Sharp brothers who became priests and went off to South America. Every now and again they would come home, their accents a little further from the East End, and tell us about their mission with the poor. We did have a sense that we connected to a much bigger family, but more in the sense of having distant cousins who needed a bit of a handout from time to time.

In the Gospels there is very little doubt about the essence of being a disciple, or what *Lumen Gentium* calls the "soul of the apostolate" (*LG*, 33). Love of God of course is the essence, as exemplified by Jesus in his intimate communion with *Abba*, his Father in heaven. But the other dimension of the Christian life, which is inseparable from this, is love of neighbour, especially the poor, the outcast, and even more radically the enemy. Jesus gives us very little room for manoeuvre here. His new commandment (*mandatum novum*) is to "love one another as I have loved you" (John 15:12). In loving our neighbour we are loving God and in ignoring the needs of our neighbour, as the unjust found out in Matthew 25, we are ignoring God. For a clear and compelling account of this fundamental truth of Christianity, we look to another of the major documents of Vatican II, *Gaudium et Spes* The Pastoral Constitution on the Church in the Modern World.

Gaudium et Spes was the only document of the Council that arose from the floor, so to speak, and was not planned in advance. James Carroll describes how at the end of the first session of the Council tensions were exposed and there was frustration among the bishops.

Cardinal Léon-Joseph Suenens addressed the assembly and called on the Council to be less preoccupied with the internal affairs of the Church but to "reach out and engage pressing questions of social justice, evangelisation, poverty, and peace". 1 He called for dialogue not only among the Church's own members and with other Christians, but with the modern world. His comments were met with sustained applause. It may seem strange to us at this distance from the Council that dialogue with the world should seem such a novel idea but when one recalls that included in Pius IX's *Syllabus of Errors* (1864) was dialogue with the modern world, the Cardinal's proposal was in fact ground-breaking.

The text begins with a memorable declaration that the "joys and hopes and the sorrows and anxieties of people today, especially of the poor and afflicted" (*GS*, 1) are shared by the disciples of Christ. It was inclusive, as we might say now; it was a reaching out to the world after a long period in which the Church was more like a fortress closed against the modern world. The motivation for this reaching out is the "divine seed" (*GS*, 3) in all people. The church would enter into "conversation" (*GS*, 3) with the modern world and more than that had a "duty in every age of examining the signs of the times and interpreting them in the light of the gospel" (*GS*, 4). This was not the Church which simply proclaimed the truth and the world could take it or leave it; this was a Church which would enter into respectful dialogue with human beings who had, in a phrase which Pope Francis would echo half a century later, an "inherent grandeur" (*GS*, 21), and a "noble calling" (*GS*, 3) as children of God. The foundation of the dignity of the human person in God is a central theme of *Gaudium et Spes* and provides us to this day with a starting point for dialogue with those who do not see the point of religion.

The text goes further than simply calling for a conversation. Jesus revealed to us that God is love and that the "fundamental law of human perfection and therefore the world's transformation is the command of love" (GS, 38). The Church is nothing if not ambitious; nothing less than the transformation of the world in love is the aim. That means that anyone who calls himself or herself a member of this Church has work to do. The current state of the world, when so many are diminished by poverty, slavery, lack of education and "whatever violates the integrity of the human person" is a "disgrace" (GS, 28) and intolerable. But the document does not just lament the state of the world, it calls on the disciples of the loving Christ to be agents of change. This has been a bone of contention ever since. For some, let's say on the left, the document does not go far enough. For others, let's say on the right, the document was too political and took the Church into social territory where it does not belong. For me, statements like the following seem clear enough:

> The Christian message is seen, then, not as discouraging them from building the world, or as leading them to neglect the wellbeing of their fellows, but as strictly obliging them to this as their duty. (GS, 34)

The syntax is somewhat laboured, but in several formulations the message is restated for the avoidance of doubt: faith stimulates us to "justice and love, especially towards the needy" (GS, 21). If a human being lacks the very basics required to lead a truly human life such as "food, clothing, shelter" (*GS*, 26) and if it takes "major changes in society" (*GS*, 26) to correct injustice then that is the business of the believer in Jesus.

Throughout history, many have reacted to injustice by calling for armed revolution as the only way to overthrow the powerful ones who sustain unjust structures for their own ends. In Jesus, there is no violence and no call to violence, so it would appear to be difficult to justify violence in his name; although many have, both oppressed and oppressors. I am acutely aware that I say that as one of the fortunate ones who has never lived under an oppressive regime and we should never condemn those who have and who have opted, often in despair, to resort to violence in pursuit of justice. God, the searcher of hearts, "forbids us to judge the inner guilt of anyone" (*GS*, 28).

> ### Gems from the Treasure Box #22
>
> Is not this the fast that I choose: to loose the bonds of injustice, to undo the thongs of the yoke, to let the oppressed go free, and to break every yoke? Is it not to share your bread with the hungry, and bring the homeless poor into your house; when you see the naked, to cover them, and not to hide yourself from your own kin? Then your light shall break forth like the dawn.
>
> The Prophet Isaiah

It is not only society that requires major changes. To make this transformation of society a reality it requires by God's grace "really new people and builders of a new humanity" (*GS*, 30). In a clear echo of the call for *metanoia* in the Gospels, the text also calls for "renewal of minds" (*GS*, 24) to bring about the transformation in society which will put an end to conditions which are so degrading of human beings. What brings about such a change of mind? For a Christian it is being possessed by the indwelling love of God, a love which deepens through prayerful encounter and helps us to gradually see the world with the eyes of Christ, the eyes of active compassion (see Emiliana's comments at the end of the chapter). A Marxist may also work for the transformation of social conditions, but his or her foundation, inspiration and sustenance will be different.

Break every yoke?

With the call of *Gaudium et Spes* to serve our neighbour and advance the universal common good we appeared to be on the verge of a new age of social action, but it didn't work out that way, at least not in the short term. In the 1970s and 80s there were a few people in the Church who were devoted to what was called Justice and Peace. I remember them at university. They had a kind of homespun look and talked about how coffee was produced. They were generally tolerated but certainly not mainstream. Social action was not a strong feature of the Church in the West after Vatican II. The reasons for that are complex and to some extent have to do with the wider geo-political realities of the Cold War. There were many in the Church who saw communism as a greater enemy than the capitalist-consumerist ideology of the West, led by America. When the two Cold War superpowers (USA and USSR) fought by proxy in places like South America, the institutional Church often sided with the American-backed right-wing regimes and was censorious of those priests and religious who sided with the left wing.

Apart from the Justice and Peace folk, I also remember a few people in the corner of student parties with guitars singing about *revolución* with some passion. These were even more "out there" in terms of risk. In most of the period following Vatican II, liberation theology (the attempt to read the Bible and Christian doctrine with the eyes of the poor) came to be regarded with some suspicion. According to Cardinal Walter Kasper, liberation theology was born in 1964 at a conference in Petropolis in Brazil that had been convened by the Latin American Episcopal Conference (CELAM). The leading lights were Gustavo Gutiérrez (see "Resources") and Lucio Gera, who was held in high esteem by Jorge Bergoglio. For the official Church it was seen as being too close to Marxism. For all those years, therefore, the Church in South America was largely out of bounds, apart from the Sharp brothers who came home with their strange Scottish-Spanish accents and talked a language that we really didn't understand.

Cardinal Kasper is careful to make the distinction between different types of liberation theology and sees a very different type in Argentina compared with much of the rest of South America. The theology which Bergoglio was familiar with, inspired by Gera, was less focused on the analysis of economic relations and more interested in the culture of the people, united by a common ethos. "It is a theology of the people and of culture... It does not want to lecture the people, but rather to listen to the people's wisdom. Therefore a higher value is assigned to popular piety." 2 This is evident in the papacy of Francis, with a determined effort to listen to the people ahead of the synods on the family and an unembarrassed promotion of forms of popular devotions. However, we should not mistake Jorge Bergoglio with the outspoken liberation theologians who stood up to oppressive regimes, often at great personal cost. His story is more complex.

During the Dirty War in Argentina from 1976 to 1983, when the country was ruled by a right-wing military junta, Bergoglio was Jesuit Provincial. An estimated ten to thirty thousand opponents of the right-wing regime "disappeared" or were tortured and killed. The left-wing opposition could be just as brutal. There are many who believe that Bergoglio did not do enough to prevent the arrest and torture of two Jesuits in his province and there are many more who believe that the Church in Argentina was too close to the ruling military junta. Paul Vallely quotes from a rare interview given by the unrepentant leader of the junta, General Jorge Rafael Videla, in which he said:

> My relationship with the Church was excellent. It was very cordial, frank and open. The Argentine Church in general, thankfully, was not carried away by the leftist Third World tendencies of the other churches of the continent.[3]

Gems from the Treasure Box #23

We who lived in concentration camps can remember the men who walked through the huts comforting others, giving away their last piece of bread. They may have been few in number, but they offer sufficient proof that everything can be taken from a man but one thing: the last of the human freedoms – to choose one's attitude in any given set of circumstances, to choose one's own way.

Viktor E. Frankl,
Man's Search for Meaning

It does not make for comfortable reading. In 2012, by then Archbishop of Buenos Aires, Bergoglio organised an apology from the bishops which expressed sorrow to all those who had been let down by the Church in those years. For many, it was not enough, but at this distance in time and space it is all too easy to arrive at self-righteous judgements. Vallely's careful and well-researched account of the time does not allow for easy positions but leaves you questioning what you would have done in similar circumstances and the answer is probably a lot less.

A safe pair of hands

South America has its twentieth-century martyrs who stood up to injustice in the spirit of Vatican II. Bergoglio is not one of them but nor is he tainted with support for the brutal regimes of the time. From the beginning of his papacy he has asked for prayers and called himself a sinner, like everybody else. He has opened a window on to the theology and stories of South America, including those whom we now regard as saints. One of the most inspirational stories, which again was somewhat muted in the Cold War years, was that of Oscar Romero, Archbishop of El Salvador, who was shot dead while saying Mass on 24 March 1980. He spoke out against the murderous regime which ruled his country and paid for his prophetic voice in blood. For years, the cause of his canonisation was blocked, but it should be noted that it was Pope Benedict XVI as much as Pope Francis who was instrumental in "unblocking" the process which led to his beatification in San Salvador in front of hundreds of thousands of people on 23 May 2015.

Maria Lopez Vigil interviewed around two hundred people over a thousand hours and published the edited transcripts in *Oscar Romero: Memories in Mosaic*. It is a remarkably vivid and at times harrowing account from eyewitnesses of the life and evolution of Oscar Romero from a "safe pair of hands" to prophet and martyr for the Gospel. When the Church in South America responded with radical enthusiasm to Vatican II at its conference at Medellín in Colombia in 1967, Romero was there as a secretary to his bishops' conference but did not share the enthusiasm. While the conference committed itself to base communities of lay people and a preferential option for the poor, Miguel Ventura recalls Romero saying that he felt "out of place" and was "the only one in the whole room wearing black". 4 He was traditional, bookish, pious, a friend of the rich as well as the poor, but not a radical.

In 1972, the military "won" the elections in El Salvador and immediately took steps to oppress opposition with curfews and martial law. In 1974, Romero was made Bishop of the Diocese of Santiago de Maria and began to learn over the next three years about the reality of life for the *campesinos*, the peasant farmers. However, when he was made Archbishop of San Salvador in 1977 he was still regarded as a conservative and his appointment had the backing of the business and political classes who ran the country and saw him as "one of theirs".[5] Shortly after his appointment, further rigged elections took place and thousands gathered to protest in the Plaza Libertad in San Salvador. Romero was told of the protests and was asked to attend, but he offered up only his prayers. When the army opened fire on the protesters, more than a hundred were killed.

For the government, many priests and religious were seen as being too close to the poor and the agitators, who were trying to organise resistance to the oppression and seek reform. The turning point for Romero was the killing of his friend Fr Rutilio Grande, a popular priest of the people, gunned down in his car along with his faithful old companion Manuel, who tried to protect him from the hail of bullets, and Nelson, the epileptic boy who sometimes rang the bells in the church. After much painful discussion Romero arrived at a striking decision: on the following Sunday, 20 March 1977, there would only be one Mass celebrated in the archdiocese, in the cathedral in San Salvador. This was seen as a provocative gesture. The Papal Nuncio was not pleased and in heated exchanges reminded Romero of what canon law said (as well as what the politics required), but Romero went ahead with the plan. Inocencio Alas says that the Mass was the moment of his conversion: "I felt the Holy Spirit descend upon him. Thousands of people were applauding him, and something rose within him. It was then that he crossed the threshold… There is baptism by water, and there is baptism by blood. But there is also baptism by the people."[6]

For the next three years, until his assassination in March 1980, he spoke out like a prophet against violence, oppression and injustice, knowing that from the day of the single Mass, the economic elite had begun an

Gems from the Treasure Box #24

Social justice is not so much a law that orders distribution. Seen from the Christian perspective, it is an internal attitude like that of Christ who, being wealthy, became poor to share his love with the poor. I hope that this call of the Church doesn't further harden the hearts of the oligarchs, rather that it moves them to conversion. Share what you are and what you have. Don't continue to silence through violence those who are extending this invitation to you; much less, continue killing those of us who are trying to see to it that there is a more just distribution of power and of the wealth of our country. And I say this in the first person because this week I got a warning that I am on the list of those to be eliminated next week. But, let it be known that it is no longer possible to kill the voice of justice.

Blessed Oscar Romero,
*Through the Year with Oscar Romero:
Daily Meditations*

open war on him, taking out adverts in the papers to criticise him, mocking him and spreading unfounded accusations. He understood that "putting ourselves on the side of the poor is going to mean a lot of bloodshed for us"[7] but he also came to the graced insight that as a follower of the poor Jesus there was nowhere else for the Church to be and he was the leader of the Church in that community. In the meantime, the violence escalated to horrific proportions, with ten to twenty dead bodies turning up every morning on the roads and back streets of El Salvador. He was warned that his life was in danger but refused to take any security measures, not wishing to put anyone else in danger. On the eve of his assassination he delivered his most outspoken sermon; speaking directly to the army he said: "I ask you, I beg you, I order you in the name of God: stop the repression."[8] He had just read out his own death sentence and the following evening, while saying Mass in the hospital chapel, he was killed by a single bullet to the heart.

A preferential option for the poor

Few of us in the West are called to martyrdom, although in many parts of the world today Christians are being slaughtered for their faith. Few of us are tested by having to live under the yolk of an oppressive and violent regime and who knows how we might act? Oscar Romero is a martyr for the faith but we should also remember the many thousands in El Salvador – priests, religious, lay leaders, ordinary lay people, men, women, boys and girls – who acted with such extraordinary bravery by standing up for truth and justice when they knew it could cost them their lives. The story of their bravery was repeated across South America and in many other places on many occasions throughout history. Our own experience of oppression is more remote, although in Europe many thousands acted with courage in taking a stand against Nazism and later communist oppression, but for most of us in the West our recent experience has been untroubled by such brutality.

That is perhaps why when talking to the twelve there was such a clear distinction on this topic between those who lived in England and those from the Philippines. For those who lived in England (seven of the twelve) social justice was less of a priority. They saw concern for one's neighbour as being fundamental to discipleship but they didn't have a language to talk about prophetic action, perhaps because the Church in the West generally has not regarded that as a priority. We have spent a lot of energy and language on the "culture wars", combating issues such as abortion and same-sex marriage, without much success it has to be said. For those I interviewed in the Philippines (five of the twelve) it was a very different story. Social action was part of their Gospel, part of the air they breathed. When you have a living memory of martial law (1972–81), when you are stepping over poverty in the street, that is understandable, although for the Church it is not a given, it is still a choice.

In the late 1960s and 70s, a number of bishops' conferences and religious orders in the developed world took their inspiration from Vatican II and declared a "preferential option for the poor". When I visited the Philippines as the guest of the Benedictine Sisters in Manila I heard about the historic reorientation of their mission priorities. The sisters had run private schools such as Saint Scholastica's in Manila with a focus on academic excellence since the beginning of the twentieth century. In 1975, under the leadership of Mother Irene Dabalus OSB, they made a declaration of their commitment to social justice. Saint Scholastica's adopted as its theme: "Education for Justice and Social Transformation". Social awareness and social involvement became an integral part of the educational process. In concrete terms this was translated into exposure to urban and rural poverty, immersion programmes and participation in mass actions. The girls in the school would indeed be able to share in the "joys and hopes and the sorrows and anxieties" (GS, 1) of the poor in their community. Academic excellence was still a priority, but was now a social responsibility, not a private aspiration. Love of neighbour was part of the programme.

Having visited Saint Scholastica's forty years after the declaration, I can confirm that the commitment to social responsibility is still very much a vibrant and central part of the life of the community. The school runs a Night School for girls between the ages of fourteen and eighteen who work during the day mostly as domestic servants. Staff give their time free and provide the girls with a way to improve their situation through education, with some going on to university. The school also runs a nearby shelter for homeless street families. Entire families are trafficked into the urban centres with the lure of employment and a better life and then abandoned. They live in carts on the streets and scavenge for plastic bottles and cardboard to make a few pesos. It is an existence very far from the dignity which Gaudium et Spes insists upon for all human beings. The families often fall prey to street gangs and the children end up in prostitution. Saint Scholastica's shelter can only take around eight families at a time but it offers food, decent hygiene, basic literacy and hope. It also engages the families in small-scale business enterprises which are free from exploitation, such as making cheese straws for sale in the school's canteen.

Girls from the school visit the shelter and, as we can see from Rebecca's testimony at the end of this chapter, it makes a profound impression on them. The students are also invited to take part in protests against corruption and injustice, something we are more reserved about in this country. I was invited to attend a "noise barrage" while I was there. Intrigued, I went along to find myself at a student protest about the violence used against the separatists in the south. Big drums were beaten above the noise of the city traffic, speeches delivered from makeshift podiums to cheers and applause, and then candles were lit and there was prayer. It was a different kind of Catholic culture, born of a different experience, but to me it felt much closer to the Gospel.

We looked in Chapter 2 at the different images of Jesus human beings have used for their own ends. In the 1960s and 70s Jesus was often depicted as the revolutionary, a kind of Che Guevara figure, hero of the insurgency. We can make Jesus many things but if we keep to the Gospel it is hard to avoid the conclusion that he was deeply troubled by the social conditions that degraded the poor. In Chapter 2 we also looked at the work of Fr Denis McBride on the parables as subversive texts, including the parable of the talents (Matthew 25:14-30). In my childhood this parable was used as an encouragement to make the most of your natural abilities. I still hear it used in this way today in school assemblies. The lazy servant buried his talent, as in academic talent or ability to play football, and was the villain of the piece. Quite how the "harsh man" who gave out the talents could have been mistaken for the loving God of Jesus I'm not sure.

McBride tells us that the parable is about money. The talent in the Hellenistic world was a unit of currency, with one talent worth about six thousand denarii, so quite a lot of money. The point of giving everybody talents while the master was away was so that they could make more money through usurious loans, which two of the servants achieve and are praised for their efforts. The third servant can therefore be seen as the hero of the parable since he breaks the cycle of exploitative moneymaking and stands up to the harsh master. McBride provides us with an interpretation of the parable which makes more sense to me than working really hard to get top grades:

> Given Jesus' instructions to his disciples on the dangers of riches (e.g. Matthew 19:23-26), the abuse of authority (Matthew 19:25-28) and respect for the little ones (Matthew 18:1-7) the parable's interpretation as a coded critique of rich landowners' abuse of their economic power would seem more consistent with Jesus' own values.[9]

Jesus did not lead a social revolution and he disappointed those who thought he was a militant messiah but he did criticise a status quo that exploited poor people and tolerated great divides between rich and poor. His criticism was often in the coded format of the parable, but that was perhaps because direct attacks on vested business and religious interests would probably have ended his ministry very abruptly. In Luke's Gospel

Jesus starts his public ministry in Nazareth by reading from Isaiah about the good news for the poor and the oppressed but they reject this message from the carpenter's son and try and throw him off the cliff. The parable was perhaps a better way of getting the message into people's consciousness without seeming like public antagonism.

As we said in Chapter 2, Jesus did not leave behind a manifesto with detailed instructions about what to do to bring about the reign of God. He revealed God's love and forgiveness, especially for the poor, in his encounters with people. He allowed sin to consume him and the Father's power lifted him up to show us that transforming love was a stronger force than sin and death. In every age his disciples have called upon his Spirit to guide them in how to interpret the signs of the times, how to be Christians in the here and now. We will probably argue until the second coming about how strongly social action should feature in our discipleship but I for one have been convinced that it is consistent with intentional discipleship.

Gems from the Treasure Box #25

The contemplative dimension of the Gospel manifests itself in an even deeper union with the living Christ and the practical caring for others that flows from this relationship.

Thomas Keating,
Open Mind, Open Heart

You cannot serve two masters

I believe that part of the problem is that we in the West have been compromised by the consumerist-capitalist system in which we live and we cannot see what is hidden in plain sight. The values of the marketplace have woven themselves into the very fabric of our being, hence we were so astonished when Pope Francis turned his back on the papal apartments and opted to live in the modest surroundings of Casa Santa Marta. This did not seem to have occurred to any pope until Francis came along. He opened his first exhortation, *Evangelii Gaudium*, by taking aim directly at the golden calf:

> The great danger in today's world, pervaded as it is by consumerism, is the desolation and anguish born of a complacent yet covetous heart, the feverish pursuit of frivolous pleasures, and a blunted conscience. Whenever our interior life becomes caught up in its own interests and concerns, there is no longer room for others, no place for the poor. (*EG*, 2)

The complacency and dulled conscience he so acutely identifies as the greatest danger for believers is what prevents so many in the developed world from regarding social responsibility as being of any importance. We have allowed Catholicism and wealth to wander hand in hand along our avenues with no comment. We have developed a powerful critique of capitalism in the social teaching of the Church before and after *Gaudium et Spes,* but the fact that this is routinely referred to as our "best kept secret" tells you enough about its place in the thinking and behaviour of mainstream Catholics. Because we have not promoted Catholic Christianity as a lifestyle, we have tolerated the uneasy cohabitation of religious belief and material gain and pleasure. We regard charity very often as a handout which has the added benefit of calming any stirrings of conscience. Fortunately, the Spirit is at work in many places and there are a number of people outside of the Church who are developing a non-ideological critique of capitalism, which many in the Church might find helpful.

192

The psychologist Oliver James has compared the values of consumerism to a virus which he dubbed *affluenza*. This virus entails "placing a high value on acquiring money and possessions, looking good in the eyes of others and wanting to be famous". 10 If you have a secular mindset you might think: "Well, that's exactly what I want, what's so bad about that?" James' thesis, based on a lot more interviews than my twelve, is that the values of "Selfish Capitalism", which give rise to *affluenza* and make you prone to anxiety and depression, do not fulfil your needs. He describes four basic needs of human beings, based on something approaching a consensus among psychologists: the need to be secure; to feel part of a community; to feel competent at something; and the need to be authentic. "Selfish Capitalism", which is more rampant in English-speaking countries, is based on the conviction that consumption and market forces can meet human needs. In purely secular terms, James is helping us to see that capitalism is not good for your emotional well-being, or as a Christian might say it is not good for your soul.

For many years of course there have been left-wing critiques of capitalism, but now we seem to be seeing a new wave of non-ideological critiques which arrive at the same conclusion; capitalism makes you miserable. The National Lottery is based on the dream of huge instant wealth. It is a seductive prospect and many workplace conversations end with the fantasy of the ultimate way out: "When I win the lottery..." It has, in many ways, replaced the notion of heavenly reward as a compelling vision of a better life. Other movements have sprung up to challenge the orthodoxy of "Selfish Capitalism" and the seductive offers of the corporate brands, such as *No Logo* from the book by Naomi Klein, and the latest phenomenon sweeping the developed world, *The Life-Changing Magic of Tidying* by Marie Kondo. (I can speak from personal experience of the life-changing impact of this book on our house since we became converts to the decluttering philosophy of Kondo.)

In a nutshell, what these movements and writers all seem to be saying, based on the experience of many people and the dramatic rise in the numbers of people suffering from emotional distress in developed countries (especially the USA), is that rampant capitalism does not make you happy because you will never be rich enough, handsome enough or famous enough – and all these things are not what you need anyway. This is where you would expect the Church to be nodding wisely and saying: "We've been telling you that for two thousand years." In some ways it has, but its own attachment to worldly goods has often undermined its own message. Richard Rohr makes the point in his talks that if you disobey the first commandment and worship at the feet of the golden calf, then you forever condemn yourself to not following the tenth commandment: "You shall not covet your neighbour's house... or anything that belongs to your neighbour" (Exodus 20:17). But most people do not seem to think that's a problem:

> In all my years as a Catholic priest hearing confession, I've never had anybody confess to violating the tenth commandment: coveting their neighbour's goods. Yet coveting goods is what our entire culture is based on! 11

That is quite a statement. It seems to have taken us a while to come back round to where we started when those early Christians gave it all away to look after the vulnerable and to live in common. We simply ignored Jesus when he talked about not serving two masters and looking for treasures that would last, rather than storing up treasures in this life. There have always been voices in the wilderness reminding us to live with less, from the Desert Fathers to Francis of Assisi. In our day, organisations like the Catholic Agency for Overseas Development (CAFOD) in the UK have consistently advocated living with less so that others might simply live.

Pope Francis has made this message central to his papacy: the rich must not only remember the poor with pity but become poor, the Church must become poor. We must enlarge our hearts and become attentive to the needs of our neighbours close at hand and far from home: "We need to pay attention to the global so as to avoid narrowness and banality. Yet we also need to look to the local, which keeps our feet on the ground" (*EG*, 234). There is a certain glamour that comes with an association with projects overseas which can become just another ego trip and a perverted form of tourism. It is harder sometimes to see the needs in front of us, especially when they are harder to detect, but being a Catholic in today's Church asks just that of us, since "the leaven of the Gospel… stimulates in the human heart the irresistible demand of dignity" (*GS*, 26).

We all have our own gifts, or charism, to contribute to the Church. Some have the courage and stamina to physically serve the poor in the most challenging environments, some have the courage and conviction to live in poverty themselves, some have the exceptional courage to stand alongside the poor against the oppressor. Most Catholics are not heroes and are on a journey of discovering or rediscovering how to follow Jesus in the Catholic Church. How they love their neighbour will depend on many things, but the fact that they *have to* in order to call themselves a Christian, if indeed they regard that as their deepest identity, is non-negotiable.

Gems from the Treasure Box #26

It may be possible for each to think too much of his own potential glory hereafter; it is hardly possible for him to think too often or too deeply about that of his neighbour. The load, or weight, or burden of my neighbour's glory should be laid on my back, a load so heavy that only humility can carry it, and the backs of the proud will be broken.

C.S. Lewis,
The Weight of Glory

Comments from the twelve on the global Church and the common good

When I was appointed I was faced with one big case of a student who just saw a phone in the room and was tempted to take it and so she did and after investigations she admitted to stealing it and when I talked to her about it you could see that it was just that she saw the phone and thought "Why don't I get it?" She has a better phone than the phone she stole. So when we talked about it, of course she was scared etc., so I asked her: "What do you want to do to make up for what happened, to correct what happened?" and she told me: "Miss, let me do something that will help me be better."

So I said: "I'll bring you to the street families, you will have to stay there for three days and you will have to work with them," and so every day she would have to report to me. She'd give the kids a bath, she taught them, she prepared them for their assignments and she also followed them wherever they went, because they live in carts, she saw how difficult life is for them. At the same time she saw the values that these children, these families had. She was telling me: "Miss, do you know that if anyone gets food, it's not something that person would eat. It's something that would be divided amongst the families. If it's just one piece of sandwich it's divided among six people."

She found that very meaningful because her father is working in Italy and she has this habit of asking for gadgets – cellphone, laptops, cameras – from her father and when she stayed there for several days she realised that she has too much compared to the street families. After that she went back, even after the three days that were required of her, and she even brought her family there because it was almost Christmas and the father came from Italy and they brought food to the family. When we were talking about it the mother was saying there was a complete change in her because she would ask for a lot of gadgets but now she was not asking for any.

Rebecca, 51, Dean of Studies

At the same time I was engaged in social work I was assigned in the community to help a number of organisations, but I thought: "I need prayer to balance all this work." Like in the Rule of Saint Benedict: work and prayer… to reflect on what I'm doing… "Is it really for the good of the community?" Only work without God and not praying doesn't sit well with me. And when I was praying I wanted the community. I consider that very precious because when I attend this I'm praying with the whole Church, praising God together in Lauds and Vespers, as if I get my strength in that. That is how I see it. You can really get lost working and working and working. There has to be a time when you recharge, when you ask "what is all this work telling me?"

Lirio, 82, kindergarden school teacher

It's hard to untangle them because your action can also enrich contemplation and your contemplation can also enrich your action. That was my quarrel with my religious superiors, especially the end of martial law. I entered the convent in 83 so there was still a lot of protest action and we would go to mobilisations and rallies and my superior general said: "Ok, be home before vespers." I said: "It's not as if I'm not praying when I'm doing this!" The prayer life has a different colour when you're in touch with this situation. People who are homeless, people have no land, no job and you begin to create your own prayer. It echoes with the psalms but this is more alive again because the lamentation is for real.

Archie, 65, religious studies teacher

You can deceive yourself a lot. You can say that you're working for people but actually you can use people for your own ego and that's why you have to have solitude so that you can really look at yourself in the mirror and say "let us see what your motivations are" and you catch yourself in your ego which is so tricky because it goes into all nooks and corners of whatever you want to do that is good. That's very important – reflection – because without that reflection you go from one activity to the other, deceiving yourself that you're doing great. All the time you are using people for your own ego.

Mary John, 78, nun

Transformation is something from the inside to the outside and yes, it's good for you, but then it needs to bear fruit and the fruit of a transformed life brings other people to God. It gives you the strength and the ability to love your neighbour as yourself and it gives you also the ability to listen to the community around you, what their needs are. You listen to the community and, because your conscience then becomes alive to God, it becomes alive to the community and therefore you start applying what you have inside – you start doing it on the outside. Starting with yourself, obviously, because it's love yourself and then love your neighbour. If you don't love yourself first, how can you love your neighbour? You love yourself by letting God love you, so once you get God's love in you and transform you, then you can start loving your neighbour. If you start loving your neighbour if you don't love yourself; it's not real love. Then that's the fruit and the fruit is whatever need the community has, so then you ask the Lord: "What do you want me to do? Where do you want me to help?"

Emiliana, 45, charity co-founder

Reflections for individuals

- What has been your own experience of social action or social responsibility? Has it played any part in your faith journey so far?

- What do you think Jesus means by the command to love your neighbour?

- Which of the Gems or which comments from the twelve on the subject of social action or love of neighbour strike a chord with you in particular? Why do you think that is?

Reflection activity for groups

- What is your community's understanding of the command to love your neighbour? What is your understanding of the needs of the local community and what you might do to help? What is your perception of the global community and what you might do to help to advance the cause of human dignity?

Suggestions for further study

Compendium of Social Doctrine of the Church: http://www.vatican.va/roman_curia/pontifical_councils/justpeace/documents/rc_pc_justpeace_doc_20060526_compendio-dott-soc_en.html. For those who wish to undertake a fuller reading of the social doctrine of the Church all the key documents were gathered together in this compendium published in 2004 at the request of Pope John Paul II.

Oscar Romero, *Through the Year with Oscar Romero: Daily Meditations* (London: Darton, Longman & Todd, 2000). To read these meditations from the final years of Oscar Romero's life is to read the witness of a transformed Christian. He was truly converted to the Gospel by the suffering of the poor and the destruction of his friends. He speaks with authority, like any true prophet, and leaves us feeling uncomfortable, as the Gospel should.

Gustavo Gutiérrez, *A Theology of Liberation*. For those who wish to look further into liberation theology this book is regarded by many as the seminal text.

CAFOD, perhaps the organisation which has done the most in this country to keep the flame of Catholic social action alive. http://www.cafod.org.uk, accessed 30 July 2015.

Poverty Statistics in the UK. The headline figures are shocking: the UK has one of the worst rates of child poverty in the industrialised world; in 2014 one in four children were classified as living in poverty. http://www.endchildpoverty.org.uk/why-end-child-poverty/key-facts, accessed 30 July 2015

The Paradox of Choice. Professor Renata Saleci, https://www.thersa.org/discover/videos/rsa-animate/2011/06/rsa-animate---choice/, accessed 30 July 2015. The RSA Animate series is a highly engaging way to discover some of the main streams of thought from today's intellectual community. The talks are around ten minutes long and the animated visuals are like the best lecture notes you never took at university. In this intriguing talk Professor Saleci explores the anxiety and dissatisfaction surrounding apparently limitless choice. Like Oliver James, she questions the benefits of consumerism and asks whether the freedom to be the architects of our lives hinders rather than helps us.

Notes

[1] *Vatican II: The Essential Texts* (New York: Random House, 2012), 189

[2] Walter Kasper, *Pope Francis' Revolution of Tenderness and Love* (New York: Paulist Press, 2015), 16

[3] Paul Vallely, *Pope Francis: Untying the Knots* (London: Bloomsbury, 2013), 119

[4] Maria Lopez Vigil, *Oscar Romero: Memories in Mosaic* (London: Darton, Longman and Todd, 1993), 38

[5] Lopez Vigil, *Oscar Romero*, 81

[6] Lopez Vigil, *Oscar Romero*, 118

[7] Lopez Vigil, *Oscar Romero*, 180

[8] Lopez Vigil, *Oscar Romero*, 399

[9] Denis McBride,C.S.sR., *The Parables of Jesus* (Chawton: Redemptorist Publications 1999), 88

[10] Oliver James, *Affluenza* (London: Vermilion, 2007), vii

[11] Richard Rohr with J. Feister, *Jesus' Plan for a New World: The Sermon on the Mount* (Cincinnati: St Anthony Messenger Press, 1996), 135

Chapter 8

God is love – reflections from the community of the Beloved Disciple

When the Church looks to the future, it often takes its inspiration from the past. This can lead to a kind of buttoned-up traditionalism which resists any prospect of change. Tradition in the best sense, however, passing on what is most precious in the life of the Church, can energise a tired generation. There have been many individuals and communities through the ages which seem to represent an authentic living out of the Gospel message of love and compassion, from the first Christian community in Jerusalem in the mid 30s AD, to the modern-day communities of Blessed Teresa of Calcutta, whose Missionaries of Charity religious order is committed to serving the poorest of the poor.

One Christian community that doesn't get much attention these days is the Community of the Beloved Disciple, the Fourth Gospel written according to tradition by John. This group probably started in Palestine along with the other Jewish-Christian communities of the middle third of the first century. It is then thought they moved out of Palestine in the 60s due to the unrest of the Jewish revolt against the Romans. They may have settled further north and west in modern- day Turkey, some say in Ephesus. This is a particularly attractive notion since Ephesus to this day still has many beautifully preserved public buildings, arches, colonnades and *agoras* from the classical era and it's not difficult to imagine a first-century figure under the very blue sky telling a curious crowd about this Lord and Saviour who came from God,

201

preached and healed, was crucified and was raised from the dead – all within living memory.

The community seems to have been joined by Gentile Christians, perhaps from the Samaritan mission, who changed the group's perspective from broadly middle of the road to something more liberal. The hero and founder of the community is the mysterious figure of the Beloved Disciple: "the disciple whom Jesus loved" (John 21:20). The American biblical scholar Raymond E. Brown, one of the great Catholic authorities on the Gospel of John, is in no doubt that

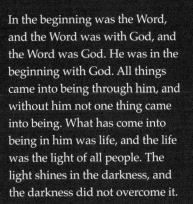

Gems from the Treasure Box #27

In the beginning was the Word, and the Word was with God, and the Word was God. He was in the beginning with God. All things came into being through him, and without him not one thing came into being. What has come into being in him was life, and the life was the light of all people. The light shines in the darkness, and the darkness did not overcome it.

The Gospel of John

the Beloved Disciple was a historical figure. The Johannine community "is one that is aware of its roots in eyewitness tradition – an awareness that supports the thesis that the Beloved Disciple was part of Jesus' following".[1] Brown does not believe that the Beloved Disciple is the author of the Fourth Gospel and in the course of his scholarly career changed his view that the author was John son of Zebedee, who was one of twelve apostles. He concludes that, as with the other Gospels, the identity of the human author is lost to history.

Brown's theory about the development of the Beloved Disciple has a compelling psychological realism. He believes that he was initially a disciple of John the Baptist, like a number of other disciples who went on to follow Jesus. He was probably not one of the twelve and became "beloved" as he matured in his faith later in life and came to penetrate the mystery of Jesus more deeply than other disciples. He appears six times in the Gospel of John and what intrigues Brown is that "in five of the six passages where he is mentioned, the Beloved

Disciple is explicitly contrasted with Peter".[2] At the Last Supper (John 13:23-26) he rests his head on Jesus (which was easy to do in the reclining positions at supper in those times). When the talk turns to betrayal an agitated Peter, who is clearly not next to Jesus, has to signal to the Beloved Disciple to find out what is going on. At the crucifixion, the contrast is implicit: Peter has denied Jesus and is nowhere to be seen, while the disciple Jesus loved is at the foot of the cross with Mary.

On the morning of the resurrection, the Beloved Disciple outruns Peter to the empty tomb, but gives Peter his place and lets him enter the tomb first. Peter sees the folded grave-clothes but it is the other disciple who "saw *and believed*" (my emphasis) (20:8). When the risen Jesus appears on the shore of the Sea of Tiberias, it is the Beloved Disciple who recognises him and says to Peter: "It is the Lord!" (John 21:7) as if to say *"will you please try and keep up?"* Peter's rehabilitation involves Jesus asking him three times if he loves him, to correct the three denials. There is no need for Jesus to ask the Beloved Disciple that question. The last straw is when Peter gets his tough-sounding commission from Jesus: "Someone else will fasten a belt around you and take you where you do not wish to go" (John 21:18). Peter points to you-know-who and says: "Lord, what about him?" (John 21:21). Jesus' answer sounds very much like "leave him alone and mind your own business", almost like a parent defending the youngest child from the unwanted attentions of the eldest: "If it is my will that he remain until I come, what is that to you?" (John 21:22).

Brown comments that "such contrasts cannot be accidental".[3] So what is going on here? This figure does not appear in any of the other Gospels and in Matthew and Luke, if not in Mark, the apostles are portrayed with much greater reverence. John certainly gives the twelve apostles their place but he does not use the term "apostle", and what Brown calls the "one-upmanship"[4] every time Peter and the Beloved Disciple are in the same scene suggests that "their man" is the disciple par excellence and more than that, the most important thing is not the office you hold in the Church but being a loving disciple; the primacy of love over the primacy of authority. When pastoral authority is conferred on Peter – "Feed my sheep" (21:17) – it is only after Peter has three times declared his love for Jesus.

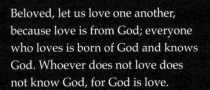

Gems from the Treasure Box #28

Beloved, let us love one another, because love is from God; everyone who loves is born of God and knows God. Whoever does not love does not know God, for God is love.

First Epistle of John

The Church had to deal with how to function as an institution from the very beginning. As numbers grew and the geographical spread widened so the need increased to hold together this growing community under some coherent identity of belief. As we saw at the Council of Jerusalem the need was felt early on for some process by which authoritative decisions could be made. We can see in the Acts of the Apostles and the Pastoral letters (I and II Timothy and Titus) a developing interest in ecclesiastical offices. This is reflected in the imagery of the body in Pauline writing, with the implication of some parts being more important than others. The same concern is also evident in Paul's hierarchy of charisms at the service of the community: "First apostles, second prophets, third teachers…"(1 Corinthians 12:28). In John the imagery is strikingly different: "The image of the vine and branches places emphasis on only one issue: dwelling on the vine or inherence in

Jesus."[5] Discipleship based on love, Brown goes on to say, "makes any other distinction in the Johannine community relatively unimportant".[6]

At the beginning of chapter 15 of John's Gospel, Jesus describes himself as the true vine and we are the branches. He says: "Abide in me as I abide in you" (15:4). If we do that we will bear fruit, but apart from him "we can do nothing" (15:5). This is a description of an ontological reality for the Christian. If we are not connected to Jesus, then we are spiritual orphans. The branches which do not abide in him wither and are thrown into the fire. That is not a threat of hellfire. That is a statement of reality *in this life*: without being connected to the vine that is Jesus we are already dead. He is our life. How we become and remain part of that life has been one of our major preoccupations.

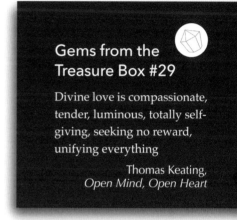

Gems from the Treasure Box #29

Divine love is compassionate, tender, luminous, totally self-giving, seeking no reward, unifying everything

Thomas Keating,
Open Mind, Open Heart

As we saw in Chapter 4, the early Christians were connected to life in Christ through a community of believers who celebrated the Eucharist, studied the teachings of the apostles, and prayed. We have developed the final point further by suggesting that for the Church today some form of contemplative prayer arising out of a study of scripture is the most transformational way to connect to the life of God. The comments from the twelve have shown their struggles to stay connected and at the end of this chapter we hear their advice for those who may feel like leaving the Church. They acknowledge that the institution of the Church, or some of its members, is sometimes the problem, and the Church itself has admitted that from time to time. But what our twelve say consistently and what John says in his Gospel is that the most important thing is to stay connected to him who is your life.

Women in the Community of the Beloved Disciple

As we have noted already, women have not always felt as if they have a place in the Church commensurate with their dignity. The role of women in John's Gospel, and therefore we assume in the community of the Beloved Disciple, is quite different from the other Gospels. You would expect that to be the case if the highest dignity is being a disciple of Jesus. That implies a profound equality of believers. In the case of the encounter between Jesus and the Samaritan woman (John 4:1-42) it is striking that not only does Jesus talk to this representative of a despised group (which makes his choice of the Good Samaritan as the hero in that parable all the more pointed) but she ends up being a missionary disciple. If this story arose from the experience of the Samaritans who joined the community of the Beloved Disciple, as many assume, then what an inspired way to make them feel welcome and valued.

It was a low-key encounter to begin with. Jesus has stopped at Jacob's Well at noon. He is thirsty, hot and tired. His disciples have gone off to buy food. A woman appearing on her own at a well at noon in those small agrarian communities is probably something of an outcast, since the women would have gone together in the cool of the morning or evening. The first remarkable thing that Jesus does is speak to her – she is a Samaritan and in the other Gospels the focus is on the lost sheep of the house of Israel. In John's community the interest has clearly widened. He offers her "living water" (4:10) which she doesn't quite understand but is curious enough (*attracted* enough?) to ask for more information. Jesus asks her to go and bring her husband and they'll have a respectable conversation, but he is gently playing with her since he knows fine well that she's had five husbands and her current partner is not her husband.

She has been looked into like clear water and she is astonished. What is perhaps more remarkable than the knowledge Jesus has of this woman's persistent attempts to find human affection and acceptance is his complete lack of judgement. It should not really come as a surprise since we see the same approach throughout the Gospels, for example

206

in the late addition to John's Gospel of the woman taken in adultery (no sign of the *man* taken in adultery, by the way, and he would be just as culpable). Jesus literally and spiritually disarms the righteous mob that is about to bury the distressed woman under a hail of palm-sized stones by inviting the sinless one to cast the first stone (see Endnote). He does not condemn her and he does not condemn the Samaritan woman. What she experiences is a conversation that should never have happened and a seeing-through that leaves her stronger, unlike the cold gaze of her community that diminishes her.

In a beautifully telling detail she leaves her empty jar behind and runs off to tell the community who have no time for her that she has met a prophet who can see beyond our sad efforts to find love and our place-bound efforts to find God. She has become an apostle, a teacher. We seem to have forgotten that so many of those who teach in the Gospels are the last, the lost and the least who have been touched by Jesus. When the disciples return from their shopping expedition they are surprised to find him speaking to a woman but sense that there is a bigger point at play here and wisely don't say anything. When the woman has run off ablaze at noon with the good news, they turn their attention to the safer topic of lunch.

Gems from the Treasure Box #30

And therefore with his grace and his help we may stand and gaze at him in the spirit, with unending amazement at this high, surpassing, inestimable love that almighty God has for us in his goodness. And therefore we may reverently ask our loving friend whatever we wish; for our natural wish is to have God, and God's wish is to have us. And we can never stop wishing or longing until we fully and joyfully possess him, and then we shall wish for nothing more; for he wants us to be absorbed in knowing and loving him until the time when we reach fulfilment in heaven.

Julian of Norwich,
Revelations of Divine Love

The apostle to the apostles

Mary Magdalene is another female character in John's Gospel who is given a prominence not found in the synoptics. She does feature in all of the Gospels as the first witness to the empty tomb. In Matthew's Gospel the risen Jesus appears to Mary Magdalene and the other Mary, but it is in John's account that the scene is played out with apostolic significance. Raymond E. Brown comments that "a key to Peter's importance in the apostolate was the tradition that he was the first to see the risen Jesus". [7] In John's account, as we have seen, Peter has already been somewhat put in his place by the fact that the Beloved Disciple sees the empty tomb and, unlike Peter, "believed" (John 20:8), although neither of them see the risen Lord. They returned to their homes but Mary, who had raised the alarm, stayed there "weeping outside the tomb" (John 20:11). It is then that Jesus appears to her and she recognises him not in the breaking of the bread but in the calling of her name, "Mary!" (John 20:16).

She is given the commission to go and tell the others and proclaims the joyful news with the standard apostolic announcement: "I have seen the Lord" (John 20:18). In Luke's Gospel the excited disciples return from Emmaus to hear that the Lord has already appeared to Peter and in Paul's formulations of the resurrection appearances (1 Corinthians 15:5) Peter (Cephas) is always given prominence but John seems to be making a point here by giving to a woman a role traditionally associated with Peter. It is perhaps the same point he is making by comparing Peter and the Beloved Disciple – that while ecclesiastical authority is important, the most important thing is being a disciple and among disciples there is equality of gender. Mary Magdalene was revered in the early Church and in the Western tradition received the honour of being the only woman, besides Mary the Mother of God, on whose feast the creed was recited because she was considered an apostle – in fact the apostle to the apostles, *apostola apostolorum*.

Somewhere along the way in the (male) tradition it was decided that Mary was a prostitute whom Jesus rescued from depravity. It does not say that anywhere in the Gospels. In the Jewish Talmud, the town of Magdala, where she came from, was condemned for harlotry, but Mary herself was never described as a prostitute. It says in Luke's Gospel that "seven demons had gone out of her" (Luke 8:2). The perfect number seven suggests that she had some kind of complete or dominating possession or condition, but whatever afflicted her, the assumption is that Jesus healed her and from that moment she followed him and helped to provide for him. In terms of the stages of discipleship we looked at in Chapter 2, she went straight from dissatisfaction to following and no wonder: if someone came into your life and lifted your great burden you would want to attach yourself to that life-giving presence.

Carelessness with her reputation led to the name of Mary Magdalene becoming synonymous with "fallen women". The first Magdalene House for such women is said to have opened in Naples in the fourteenth century. Magdalene Laundries (or asylums) were still functioning in Ireland until as recently as 1996, run by religious orders of nuns. Young girls and women were sent to these penal institutions for redemption and correction by the courts, the parishes and embarrassed Catholic families because they had in some way broken the sexual mores of the community, or because they had learning needs the community could not meet. They also provided a source of free (slave) labour for the many hotels and church organisations that used the laundry service.

Physical and emotional abuse was widespread and unchecked until the scandal broke in Ireland with the discovery of a mass grave at one of the laundries in 1993. A formal state apology was finally issued in 2013 by Enda Kenny, the Irish Taoiseach (Prime Minister), and a £50 million compensation scheme was set up. In a statement to the Irish Parliament, with survivors from the laundries present in the public gallery, he said that: "By any standards it was a cruel and pitiless Ireland, distinctly lacking in mercy." [8] There was a standing ovation, for the survivors. The four religious orders that ran the laundries have also issued apologies but have so far been reluctant to contribute to the compensation scheme. The film *The Magdalene Sisters* (2002), written and directed by Peter Mullan, was based on the accounts of four survivors from one of the laundries. It is a powerful and harrowing account of what happened in these institutions.

It is a challenge to the faith and commitment of Catholics when such terrible, systematic wrongs are revealed. It is a challenge not to walk away, but to resist and reform the mindset which could lead to the existence of such places. Taking their name from a perverted interpretation of the first female apostle, the Church allowed such places to thrive for hundreds of years. The Church at times can be overly defensive about such revelations, but it cannot be denied that over many years the Church tolerated the abusive treatment of girls and women due to a punitive theology of sin and redemption which located much of the responsibility for sexual temptation and activity upon women.

The community inspired by the Beloved Disciple seems to have practised a radical counter-cultural equality. It is far from clear if women were "presbyters" or priests but it is remarkable that in John's Gospel the role of the person who declares the identity of Jesus, again normally reserved for Peter (Matthew 16:16), goes to a woman. Martha, the sister of Mary and Lazarus, says to Jesus: "I believe that you are the Messiah, the Son of God" (John 11:27). The inspiration for this community was the Beloved Disciple and it was characterised by a pure and sustained focus on Jesus as the gift of God. The community suffered a painful separation from "the Jews" (that is the Jewish community of the time, not Jews of all time) over its understanding of the divine origin

Gems from the Treasure Box #31

Jesus puts us His hearer in the role of the father, of the one who forgives. Because if we are, so to speak, the debtor (and of course we are that, too), that suggests no graciousness in us. And grace is the great gift. So to be forgiven is only half the gift. The other half is that *we* also can forgive, restore and liberate, and therefore feel the will of God enacted through us, which is the great restoration of ourselves to ourselves.

Marilynne Robinson,
Gilead

of Jesus and the text is marked by the experience of public argument and counter-argument with the other group. However, what emerged so strongly is the great revelation that God is love and "everyone who loves is born of God and knows God" (1 John 4:7). *Everyone who loves.*

The face of mercy

When Pope Francis called for a Year of Mercy in 2015–16 he was clearly determined to keep our minds focused on the heart of divine revelation. *Misericordiae Vultus*, The Bull of Indiction of the Extraordinary Jubilee of Mercy opens with the words: "Jesus Christ is the face of the Father's mercy."[9] The timings of the year are significant. The Holy Door (of mercy) was opened on 8 December 2015, the fiftieth anniversary of the closing of the Second Vatican Council. The Pope feels a pressing need to "keep this event alive"[10] in the minds of the faithful. He acknowledges the significance of the Council when "the walls which for too long had made the Church a kind of fortress were torn down and the time had come to proclaim the Gospel in a new way."[11] The *kerygma* may be proclaimed in a new way but it is the same evangelisation we have known from the beginning. The heart of that evangelisation, the heart of the revelation, the Pope is in no doubt, is the mercy of God.

He reminds us that his predecessor Blessed Paul VI, speaking at the close of the Council in 1965, said that the Good Samaritan was "the model of the spirituality of the Council".[12] The story of the outsider who stooped in pity to the wounded stranger on the side of the road is held up by the Church as the model of a spirituality for our times. There is, for some, a shocking element to this choice. The story does not even mention God, or belief systems, or membership of a church. The response of loving care to a vulnerable brother is seen as what God in Jesus regards as the test of our humanity. The unmerciful and cautious response of the clerics who walked past the bleeding man is forever a source of discomfort for those who claim to represent religion. I vividly remember hearing a member of a religious order saying in a public lecture that since Francis became pope he has not been able to walk past a homeless person in the street, implying that before Francis, like the priest in the parable, that is exactly what he did.

The other parables which Pope Francis invites us to consider in *Misericordiae Vultus* are the parables of mercy in chapter 15 of Luke's Gospel: the lost sheep, the lost coin and the lost son, more popularly known as the parable of the prodigal son. He calls these parables "the core of the Gospel",[13] which is a clear invitation to any disciple to make these parables an object of particular reflection. The short parables of the lost sheep and coin have some parallels in the other synoptic Gospels but the parable of the lost son is Luke's unique contribution to the tradition. In Chapter 2 we looked at the parables as texts which undermined the values of the time which supported injustice and corruption, usually at the expense of the most vulnerable. In considering the parable of the prodigal son, Denis McBride reminds us of the context of all three of the parables of mercy. The chapter begins with two distinct audiences coming to Jesus: the tax collectors and sinners, who "were coming near to listen to him" (Luke 15:1), and the Pharisees and the scribes who were complaining that "This fellow welcomes sinners and eats with them" (Luke 15:2).

The context then is a response to the religious authorities of the day who are opposed to Jesus' strategy of unconditional table fellowship. Earlier on in Luke's Gospel we have already seen how little the Pharisees have to offer to sinners, when Simon the Pharisee cannot even acknowledge the existence of the woman who burst into his dinner party to cover the feet of Jesus with kisses. Why does she behave this way? Because she had been forgiven. The great weight of her sins – "which were many" (Luke 7:47) – had been lifted. The Pharisee has no ministry for this woman. He believes in separation of the clean from the unclean until the unclean see fit to change their ways and then the separation might be overcome. Jesus does not lay down preconditions for his forgiveness but as McBride observes: "Love and forgiveness are offered in the hope that change and renewal will be the outcome; love and forgiveness are not, therefore, a reward for conversion."[14] As Pope Francis reminds us, this is not just the strategy of a remarkable prophet who had a gift for making people feel valued, this is the very nature of God since "Jesus of Nazareth, by his words, his actions, and his entire person reveals the mercy of God."[15]

Scholars will tell you that when the prodigal son asked his father for his share of the inheritance it was tantamount to wishing him dead. It just wasn't done in those days and would have brought disgrace on the whole family. The prodigal's plan for dissolution in a foreign land soon unravels when misfortune arrives in the form of a famine, the bank account is empty, and he ends up working in a pigsty, literally. The prodigal has some sense that his father might take him back (he already knows he is not harsh) and has his speech ready: he'll work as a hired hand, anything but this existence with the pigs, the lowest of the low for a Jewish audience. The poignant and telling point about the story is that the father (God the Father) does not sit in his pomp waiting for his errant son to deliver his grovelling speech.

While the boy was still some way off, his father "saw him and was filled with compassion" (Luke 15:20). This middle-aged man who has been embarrassed by his testosterone-filled son (and what father hasn't?) then "ran" (Luke 15:20) and embraced his boy. This was very undignified behaviour for a Middle Eastern man. The son doesn't quite get to the bit in his speech about being a hired hand because he doesn't get a chance. His father is babbling out orders to the servants to bring the best robe, a ring and sandals for his feet (a sure sign of the son's dignity restored). Compassion is the main characteristic of God as revealed in the parables. We often hear that Jesus looked upon the crowds with compassion. But this is not a kind of aloof pity. Jose Pagola, among others, comments on the Greek word for compassion used by the evangelists: "The writers use a very expressive Greek word, *splanjnizomai*, which literally means that Jesus' (and God's) 'bowels shook' when they saw people suffering." [16] Pope Francis seems to have the same thing in mind when he describes the mercy of God not as an "abstract idea" but a "visceral love" which "gushes forth from the depths naturally".[17]

The image of God cramping in his gut with pity for us goes to the heart of the mystery of the human condition. There are those who say spare us the pain in the first place. There are others who derive great comfort from knowing that they are never beyond the compassion of

God. In the parable, the return of the son is marked by wild celebrations. The father orders more than a takeaway for the welcome-home supper: the "fatted calf" (Luke 15:23) would have been reserved for a special feast and the implication is that the whole community would have been invited. There is no question of any conditions attached to the son's return to table fellowship. He does not have to prove that he is good or worthy, or that he won't do this again – the point is that the father is good and full of mercy. That is what we are invited to believe about God and for so long have struggled to do so.

Henri Nouwen in *The Return of the Prodigal Son* makes the connection between the prodigal son's departure from his home and the human experience we all have in common of leaving the "home" of our True Self and taking our chances in the turmoil of a mind in thrall to the world and its expectations. In Chapter 6 we looked at the reclamation of the contemplative tradition which many in the Church now see as the way to renewal. We spend most of our conscious lives in the realm of the "False Self"; the "distant country" of a mind which obsessively and compulsively processes reality according to either our own deeply embedded hurts and drives or what we consider to be "important" in the eyes of others. Existence in this country cannot ultimately provide any contentment for us and we will sooner or later, either literally or metaphorically, end up in the depths of the pigsty. Our "home" is our life in God which is available to us in the True Self. There is a great allure in the distant country. It is harder to stay at home and experience the deep reality of our beloved status. As Nouwen comments: "Why do I keep ignoring the place of true love and persist in looking for it elsewhere? Why do I keep leaving home where I am called a child of God, the Beloved of my Father?"[18]

One of the problems Nouwen identifies is that we don't actually seem to want God's forgiveness, or to live in the True Self (one implies the other). The prodigal was inspired not so much by repentance but by the depravity of his circumstances. He just wanted a better deal. Most of us seem to be happier to carry the burdens of unforgiveness, to live in the drama of the False Self, than to enter into an exchange of mercy (given and received) which would see us come out the other end transformed. Nouwen comments that "receiving forgiveness requires a total willingness to let God be God and do all the healing, restoring and renewing".[19] In the Catholic culture where we started our journey the practice of weekly confession was common. You would kneel in the darkness of the confessional and tell the profile of the priest through the grille your sins of the week. It was a sacramental way of experiencing the forgiveness of God but like many of the practices of that culture it has fallen away and is now in the process of being reclaimed by a more adult understanding of reconciliation.

The wider secular culture again has much to teach us in this respect. There have been many extraordinary stories of forgiveness and reconciliation in recent years. The instant access to such stories on digital networks has been a great bonus. The Forgiveness Project is a website that collects stories of forgiveness and reconciliation from around the world, irrespective of religious affiliation. It is at times very difficult to read. You feel you are on the very frontier at times of the human condition. To give or receive forgiveness you need to be at an emotional and spiritual depth which few of us experience outside of heartbreak. We have much to learn from these brave people about the psychology of forgiveness which will throw light on the theology. In the confessional it was like a transaction, carried out by formula. I said the right words and I received absolution. I put my card in the ATM and money came out. I sometimes felt better for a while but then soon went about committing the same sins again. I think this is why so few took this practice into adulthood, or even into mid-teens. There was such a lack of understanding of what is going on.

Forgiveness is forgiveness, whether it's in first-century Palestine or twenty-first-century Rwanda. The psychology is the same. If unforgiveness keeps us locked in guilt as a perpetrator, or resentment as a victim (like the elder son in the parable), then a grace-filled convulsive movement of the spirit is required to either forgive or be forgiven. The levee breaks and the release of emotion threatens to overwhelm us as grace pours in and through our parched landscape. Was this not what the woman in Luke's Gospel experienced after her encounter with Jesus? She couldn't stop crying and gatecrashed the party to show love for this man who released her from the sinful identity in which her religion and community wanted to keep her. The Forgiveness Project has many stories which refer to the same phenomenon, working in both directions. Jean-Baptiste Ntakirutmana's mother was killed in the genocide in Rwanda in 1993. In 2009 he met the man who killed her:

> When he started explaining how he killed her,
> I partly lost consciousness and Joseph carried
> on the conversation with him. I prayed to

> God to revive me and give me more strength
> to continue, as I felt this was my mission.
> Miraculously I then felt warmth spread from
> my head to my feet. I felt a big rock melting
> from my chest and head. I felt very refreshed.
> I cleaned up my tears and carried on the
> conversation, feeling tremendously relieved
> throughout my whole being.[20]

We need to forgive as well as be forgiven to take part in the life of God which is a continual pouring out of love and compassion. Saint Paul calls this reconciliation with God (see Gems #33) and says this is the reason Jesus became flesh. He says that we *are* reconciled to God. Jesus has accomplished that. He has blessed and forgiven reality. The Father has embraced *the whole of prodigal humanity*. It is profoundly ok. Now we need to *be* reconciled, to act like it's true. Before that revelation we did not know for sure the full nature of God. The Old Testament certainly contains many references to a God of tenderness who is slow to anger and rich in mercy but there is also vengefulness and a fierce focus at times on the law. Jesus left us in no doubt about the nature of God and didn't just tell us stories about this great truth, he showed us by the way he treated those burdened with sin, men and women, the wicked and warped, those who thought there was no way back for them.

Some people are led to profound insights about the nature of God and reconciliation (although not all refer to God) through tragedy, which seems to either make or break the human spirit. For most of us the path is thankfully more ordinary and requires the daily discipline (*ascesis*) of prayer and meditation, supported by the sacraments, the process by which we slowly discover our true selves and find ourselves somehow *changing*: becoming a little less self-absorbed, less judgemental, less sensitive to criticism, less inclined to score points or harbour hurts, more patient, more mindful of our neighbour, nicer to the people we live with, more attentive and attuned to the spiritual reality in which we are embedded. In summary: more loving.

Gems from the Treasure Box #32

A thought transfixed me: for the first time in my life, I saw the truth as it is set into song by so many poets, proclaimed as the final wisdom by so many thinkers. The truth – that love is the ultimate and highest goal to which man can aspire. Then I grasped the meaning of the greatest secret that human poetry and human thought and belief have to impart: *The salvation of man is through love and in love.* I understood how a man who has nothing left in this world still may know bliss, be it only for a brief moment, in the contemplation of his beloved. In a position of utter desolation, when man cannot express himself in positive action, when his only achievement may consist in enduring his sufferings in the right way – an honorable way – in such a position man can, through loving contemplation of the image he carries of his beloved, achieve fulfilment. For the first time in my life I was able to understand the meaning of the words: "The angels are lost in perpetual contemplation of an infinite glory."

Viktor Frankl,
Man's Search for Meaning

Being a Catholic in today's Church

Being a Catholic in the Church today is not always a comfortable experience. The Catholic Church in the West has been in decline in recent years, if measured by Mass attendance, and certainly in decline against the more nebulous but powerful measure of credibility. As society becomes more secular and less "churched" it becomes harder to even begin a conversation that relies so much on what is invisible to the eye. As the full range of behaviour in the Church over the years is exposed to the light of day, many Catholics feel on the ropes against a barrage of accusation. With the decline of the ordained clergy there seems less resource to support people in an adult faith in this challenging context. Hope has been dim at times but never extinguished. Lay people are stirring, the Church is changing, although the timescale is not modern corporate.

In the film *The Cardinal* (1962) one of the characters says: "The Church thinks in centuries." That strikes me as being very true. The Church is changing – not in its core beliefs but in the way its members seek to live out Christian lives. We were for so very long dependent on clergy to lead us to God and now the clergy are old and very few people seem to be interested in the path to ordination which I embarked on – and then left – nearly forty years ago. But God will not abandon his Church and it is no coincidence that the voices of lay preachers and teachers can be heard bringing forward ideas and programmes for a new kind of life in the Church – whether it's intentional disciples, or the signs of a dynamic Catholic or the emerging Church, there is a movement under way to reform the Church and show people how to live more like Christians within the Catholic Church.

For many it has all come too late and the lack of adult formation has allowed many to drift away. People tend not to leave the Church in a dramatic fashion, unless they live in one of the southern German states where people pay taxes to the Church from their salary. For most it's a kind of shake of the head, having had enough, having heard one story too many of abuse and damage, having been personally hurt or in extreme cases abused, or just having lost any excitement about the message. I asked the twelve to offer advice to those who consider themselves on the threshold of the Church and below you will find their responses. The twelve are certainly not apostolic saints but ordinary men and women whose journeys of faith have not been straightforward. In my own experience, I have come and gone across the threshold in both directions several times, losing interest and then finding it again. The scandals of recent times have been a real test of faith for me, a real darkness. Once I asked a dear friend and priest what we were supposed to do faced with this onslaught of unchristian behaviour. He said: "Just stay connected, hang in there." And sure enough God comes along disguised as a fellow traveller and a conversation sparks off the embers.

Being a member of the Church is to belong to a huge family, the communion of saints to use the theological term. You wouldn't want to meet every member of the family at an annual reunion, but that's probably true of all families. There is a great reservoir of wisdom as well as folly, heroes as well as howlers, but mostly just ordinary pilgrims trying to make sense of it all. Many have reflected deeply on the life, death and resurrection of Jesus and what it means for their age. You may feel that in your own corner of the country there is not much going on, it's all a bit quiet and parochial in the worst sense, but when you connect to the global family of the Church and then connect back to the history of the Church you will experience the community, the frayed *koinonia* which has survived for two thousand years. From the very beginning the Church realised the importance of community and establishing the credal bounds which defined those who belonged to the community.

A friend of mine once took me to visit his church, an independent evangelical community in the city centre. They were gathered for prayers at midday from all walks of life, young and old. They sang with passion, expressing their faith freely in their faces and bodies. Some spoke in tongues, prayed spontaneously, much to my discomfort. However, I was very moved when my friend, their pastor, read the words of Jesus at the Last Supper and then passed around fresh bread rolls and a chalice of wine. It's as if they were starting from scratch and I was intrigued that they wanted some form of Eucharist. It wasn't that long ago when it would have been a sin for me even to be there. We have spent a long time arguing and fighting over formulations of belief and defending our positions with hardening of attitude. But in my own mind I keep coming back to the thought that without some authority the centre will not hold, the group will split and split according to its own interpretations. Perhaps I just think that because of my religious background as a cradle Catholic. Perhaps I think that way because I was brought up in a left-wing political atmosphere which valued collectivism.

I do feel very strongly that we have been entrusted with a treasure in clay jars and we are asked not to keep it to ourselves. The world needs this treasure and we have been told since Vatican II and again very strongly by Pope Francis to find new ways to tell the world about our treasure in a new evangelisation. We have not always succeeded in convincing people of our good news. In 2009, Intelligence Squared hosted a debate in London on the motion "The Catholic Church is a Force for Good". [21] Stephen Fry and Christopher Hitchens spoke with great passion against the motion. Most of what they said I found myself agreeing with. They did dwell on the egregious wrongs of the Church but they are undeniably true, littered across history, and we would do well not to be so defensive about them. Stephen Fry's final point was very telling. He said that if the carpenter Jesus of Nazareth came back today he would be very uncomfortable with the pomp and wealth of the Church. I think he was right. A lot of people love Jesus but just don't get the Church. The motion was heavily defeated. It is very sad that so many people do not see Jesus when they look at the Church.

The narrative of revolution we are used to involves the violent upheaval of the old order, which has become so oppressive that armed resistance is the only path. For many in Palestine in the first century this was their hope for Jesus, but the kingdom he talked about did not involve violence or replacing one power system with another. We are only very slowly coming to terms with Jesus and what he means for the human race. There have always been those who really got it and lived as if they were disciples of Jesus. You can tell who they are by their simple lives, their compassion, their non-violence, their determination to help the poor, the time they spend in prayer. You can tell them by their love: the vanguard of the revolution of tenderness. The rest of us kind of shuffle along, hoping one day for conversion, or perhaps living quietly in fear of such a life-changing summons.

Gems from the Treasure Box #33

It was God who reconciled us to himself through Christ and gave us the work of handing on this reconciliation. In other words, God in Christ was reconciling the world to himself, not holding men's faults against them, and he has entrusted to us the news that they are reconciled. So we are ambassadors for Christ; it is as though God were appealing through us, and the appeal we make in Christ's name is: be reconciled to God.

St Paul,
Second Letter to the Corinthians

Final comments from the twelve for those on the threshold of the Church, either on the way in or the way out.

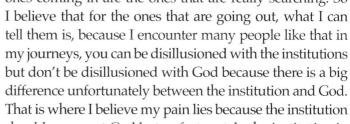

I think the ones that are going out are the ones that are disillusioned by the Church – they are hurt – and the ones coming in are the ones that are really searching. So I believe that for the ones that are going out, what I can tell them is, because I encounter many people like that in my journeys, you can be disillusioned with the institutions but don't be disillusioned with God because there is a big difference unfortunately between the institution and God. That is where I believe my pain lies because the institution should represent God but unfortunately the institution in many areas is becoming a "god" of its own and that god hurts a lot of people, that's why they leave. However, a lot of people that come in are searching for God, our God, our Lord, and they go there and many of them find it but a lot of them don't.

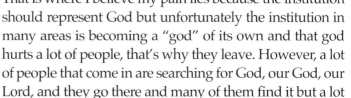

Emiliana, 45, charity co-founder

I was just thinking, for those on the way out I want to say to them "look again, turn again", because, first of all, most people who are on the way out – if they're genuine and it's not just because it's inconvenient or they've better things to do on a Sunday or something – it's because they've been hurt in some way or disappointed by the Church and I think that there is a real need for us to recognise and for them to articulate that pain or disappointment. But I think that the Church is so beautiful, is such a source of love and compassion, why would you not want to cling to it? Yes, you'll find the damaged bits, yes, you'll find the hypocrisy, yes, you'll find the terrible history of abuse we've uncovered. But actually the Church is more than

225

that and, rather than leaving, I think there's the vocation to build this Church again. I think that's the way I'd want to go on that.

For those who are staying, it's the same vocation; to love the Church in all its forms but particularly to love. For me one of the great things is the widow's mite. For me the great challenge is, we can see the popes and we can see the great liturgies in our cathedrals but for me the real mystery of the Church is that widow that nobody sees but Christ sees. She is giving what appears to us to be nothing yet it's everything. If we can touch that mystery and see that widow, then we're touching the heart of the Church.

James, 64, religious order

The Church that we believe in is so much bigger than any one of the individuals that you may encounter as representing the Church, especially when you have a real bad encounter. It's to be able to go over that negative encounter with those who have been on the receiving end of some bad people in the Church, being treated rudely or even abused. Be able to look beyond that experience and say this encounter does not represent the Christ that I believe in or that's supposed to be represented by this Church. We have to be very open-minded that this Church or the people representing the Church, just like any other representation, may not be a real representative of the faith so that when we experience that bad encounter we can get over that because some, when they have that negative encounter, walk away.

I remember an insight from a human resource conference I attended, which was that employers do not leave because of their institution, they leave because of the bad managers. It's the same with the Church. We all want to be part of the Church but some leave because of some bad managers of the Church and it's impossible to get rid of all the bad managers so it will be a constant fight. The fight between good and evil exists even within our own Church, even within our minds. It's a constant battle, a never-ending battle, and we should always pray for grace that in this battle we will be given the grace to be able to decide what is the right path.

Jun, 52, electronics engineer and whistle-blower

If they go out from the Church they will be on their own because they will not have those parameters any more, their parameters are now wider. They will have to be more reflective, they will have to be more discerning, because this time their only guide would be themselves and they have to be very honest thinkers.

Archie, 65, teacher of religion

I have relatives who are about to leave the Church. I have a niece who does not believe in marriage but I feel you can't impose belief, religion cannot be imposed. What I feel is that it's really about giving support – whatever their decisions are – because in giving support you also show who you are and what kind of religion you have. I have a sister who's very conservative and she feels very bad about my niece who's not going to Mass any more and does not believe in marriage etc., and to a certain degree she treats her differently and we would say "no, all the more we should be with her because she's going through difficult times, with her family, so the more we should be supporting". I think in that way we are showing what Catholicism is all about. It's not having lectures or seminars in relation to that, but it's the kind of support that we give that will show what we believe in, what is our religion.

Rebecca, 52, Dean of Studies

I think for those on the way out, particularly, I would say be very honest with yourself because when you read the reasons for people going you very often feel that they've left the Church a long time before and they're looking for an excuse. The imperfections of one priest, perhaps only one, then maybe several, a general attitude, a scandal and so on. You wouldn't leave your golf club because of one individual. Being honest, on the way out, what are your real reasons?

Tom, 78, retired housemaster

You know, the stuff that puts you off coming in or makes you want to go out probably isn't Catholicism.

Wendy, 52, teacher

My advice would be not to be afraid of being the person of faith that you think that you should be. Especially for young people, there is so much stigma around religion – Catholicism in general I think – because of a lot of their views towards sex before marriage and homosexuality. And as a young person you're trying to figure out who you are and what you believe, at a point when everyone around you is doing all those things that on one side you're being told is wrong and on the other side you think everyone else is doing it so why shouldn't I? It's about thinking that actually faith is personal and for me it was realising that going to church is quite a public act and I think you can go to church, be taken to church by your parents as a young person, without really having any faith. But my advice would be to think personally about what matters to you and, if what matters to you is your faith and is your religion and you've got a set of values and beliefs that are really important to you, no one else needs to worry about those. It's not their concern, it's your concern, it's what matters to you and it's what drives and inspires your life and that's really helped me to quietly become a lot closer to God and to the Church.

Xita, 20, student

The vast majority of young people are very open and friendly so I'd like to think that when my generation does get a bit older we will be open to other things and respectful so I hope there is still a place for Christianity in this country, but I think that's something we've got to fight for. In the end when it comes down to it the people in the pew who are going to care about this are going to have to be involved. As I've said to you all the way through, the days of sitting at the back and getting your card stamped are over because it doesn't work like that any more. But there's a lot of hope – I don't think we can allow ourselves to be all doom and gloom all the time because actually we might as well just go home and forget about it but I think we're all still here, we're still growing, there are great people coming in.

Paul, 23, chaplaincy assistant

Reflections for individuals

- Who is your hero or Beloved Disciple who most embodies the depth of the Gospel?

- Which of the Gems from the treasure box speaks more powerfully to you – perhaps you'd like to go back and read it again as a meditation?

- Do any of the comments from the twelve strike a chord with you? Which ones? Why?

- What are your next steps now?

Reflection activity for groups

- Who is the hero of your group or community, who is your Beloved Disciple?

- What is the place and role of women in your group?

- Would you say that your group is characterised by love and mercy? How is this shown?

- What is next for your group or community?

Resources for further study

Julian of Norwich, *Revelations of Divine Love* (London: Penguin Books, 1998). In the history of Christianity there are many Beloved Disciples who seemed to penetrate the heart of the mystery of God more than others. For those who do not have the time for a comprehensive study programme it might be advisable to get to know just one of the great mystics. In 1337, Julian received a series of "showings" or revelations of the mystery of Christ's suffering. She received assurance of God's unwavering love for humankind and his infinite capacity for forgiveness. The quotation on the back cover of the Penguin edition is particularly apt for the theme of this chapter: "Just because I am a woman, must I therefore believe that I must not tell anyone about the goodness of God?"

The Forgiveness Project, http://theforgivenessproject.com/. This remarkable website contains the stories of many ordinary people who have taken the extraordinary step of forgiving those who have hurt them, often in extreme ways. For a man to forgive the killer of his mother, for a former prisoner of war to forgive his torturer, or parents to forgive the unrepentant killer of their son requires a grace which few of us can imagine but these people have found that grace and have shown the face of mercy to the world.

Matthew Kelly, *The Four Signs of a Dynamic Catholic* (Boston: Beacon Publishing, 2014). Another key book in what seems to be a growing renewal movement in the Church, as we try to define our existence beyond the Catholic culture many of us grew up with. The four signs are not dissimilar to what we found in *Acts* – prayer, study, generosity and evangelisation.

Catechism of the Catholic Church: http://www.vatican.va/ archive/ENG0015/_INDEX.HTM, accessed 31 May 2015. I have been more focused on the *kerygma* than the *didache*, the compelling summary of the Gospel rather than the developed teaching which flows from that source. Those who wish to learn more about the teaching of the Catholic Church will find the most comprehensive and authoritative coverage in the Catechism.

Notes

[1] Raymond E. Brown, *The Community of the Beloved Disciple: The Life, Loves and Hates of an Individual Church in New Testament Times* (New York: Paulist Press, 1979), 32

[2] Brown, *Community of the Beloved Disciple*, 82

[3] Brown, *Community of the Beloved Disciple*, 83

[4] Brown, *Community of the Beloved Disciple*, 84

[5] Brown, *Community of the Beloved Disciple*, 87

[6] Brown, *Community of the Beloved Disciple*, 87

[7] Brown, *Community of the Beloved Disciple*, 189

[8] Enda Kenny, http://www.bbc.co.uk/news/world-europe-21510281, accessed 23 July 2015

[9] Pope Francis, *Misericordiae Vultus* [The Face of Mercy], 1 http://w2.vatican.va/content/francesco/en/apost_letters/documents/papa-francesco_bolla_20150411_misericordiae-vultus.html, accessed 3 May 2015

[10] Pope Francis, *Misericordiae Vultus*, 4

[11] Pope Francis, *Misericordiae Vultus*, 4

[12] Pope Francis, *Misericordiae Vultus*, 4

[13] Pope Francis, *Misericordiae Vultus*, 9

[14] Denis McBride C.Ss.R., *The Parables of Jesus* (Chawton: Redemptorist Publications, 1999), 125

[15] Pope Francis, *Misericordiae Vultus*, 1

[16] Jose Antonio Pagola, *Jesus: An Historical Approximation* (Miami: Convivium Press, 2009), 108

[17] Pope Francis, *Misericordiae Vultus*, 6

[18] Henri Nouwen, *The Return of the Prodigal Son* (London: Darton, Longman and Todd, 1992), 43

[19] Nouwen, *The Return of the Prodigal Son*, 53

[20] The Forgiveness Project, http://theforgivenessproject.com/stories/jean-baptiste-ntakirutimana-rwanda/, accessed 20 July 2015

[21] Intelligence Squared Debate (2009): *The Catholic Church is a Force for Good.* https://www.youtube.com/watch?v=dBSH2oWVGEs, accessed 23 July 2015

Christ and the Adulteress by Lucas Cranach the Younger (c. 1532, oil on copper transferred from wood 1770), Hermitage Museum, St Petersburg, Russia

John 8:1-11

Consider the hands. To the left of Jesus is the "cunning accuser", the one who can marshal the arguments. His purpose is not just to stone to death the woman caught in adultery but to "test" Jesus so they could bring a charge against him: two birds with one stone.

The law, says the cunning accuser, demands that "such women" be stoned to death. It does indeed, although he overlooks the fact that the law applies to both men and women. So where is he, Mr Tail-Between-His-Legs? Is he in the picture? Is that him by any chance in the very top left-hand corner, having a peak, perhaps drawn back by a tug of guilt?

If Jesus does not support the law, as applied narrowly by these smug and self-righteous men, then he is condemned.

233

If he supports the law, then he would be in trouble with the Romans for taking the law into his own hands. *"What will it be, Jesus?"* asks the cunning accuser in his ear, *"palm out for stoning, or palm in for not?"*

Consider the hands of the "demon accuser", further to the left. He is drooling already at the thought of such sport first thing in the morning. The subtle arguments are sailing over his head. He just wants to get started. In his right hand he clutches a palm-sized stone and in his left he holds the bucket with more.

The right hand of Jesus points to the woman as he looks at them, *"If you haven't sinned then go ahead, throw the first stone."* His right hand does more than point – it looks like the downward sweep of a blessing, the woman's head bowed to receive. The stakes are high. Will this get through the hellish mist in the mind of the demon accuser?

When the eye has consumed the drama of heads and hands it finally alights on the left hand of Jesus, holding the woman by the right hand. In other versions of this painting Jesus holds the woman by the wrist, as you might with a naughty child. Here, he holds her hand; the only male tenderness in the scene.

Where is her left hand? It seems to be lost in the folds of her dress but the arm is angled upwards, the hand reaching up to the upper left arm of Jesus. She is leaning on him, the way her head almost leans on his left shoulder.

In the bottom right-hand corner is the metallic gleam of male violence: a hammer, the handle of a sword, an echo of the stones on the other side, the implements men have used to batter, cut and crush anybody who was outside of the law, the family, the tribe, or sometimes just for the hell of it.

The penny drops, the stones drop. They are disarmed by the clarity and force of love, this time. Even the demon accuser backs down, although he is surely the last to drop his stones and will leave with a fiendish sneer, as if to say you haven't seen the last of me.

Jesus has been able to protect the woman from the violence of men, but in the end he will not be able to protect himself. His friends will take to the hills, the demon accuser will return at the head of another group of men with torches. He will be led away, whipped venomously, and lifted up in excruciating pain.

That would be the end of tenderness and the men would chunter on in their schemes, looking for their next victim with no notion of another way, were it not for that morning when another woman who had been held by the hand, whose affliction had been lifted, went to the tomb and found it empty.

She was distressed when he said *don't touch me*, but she will come to understand very soon that the touch has been transformed and is now universal: in bread and the sip of wine, in the word that sets hearts on fire, in the tight embrace of reconciliation. The revolution of tenderness had begun.

1: Hans Urs von Balthasar, *The Grain of Wheat* (San Francisco: Ignatius Press, 1995)

2: Heythrop Institute for Religion, Ethics and Public Life, *On the Way to Life* (London: Catholic Education Service, 2005)

3: Evelyn Waugh, *Letter to Edward Sackville-West,* http://www.catholicauthors.com/waugh.html, accessed 25 July 2015

4: Blessed Oscar Romero, *Through the Year with Oscar Romero: Daily Meditations* (London: Darton, Longman & Todd, 2006)

5: H.G. Wells, *A Short History of the World* (London: Penguin Classics, 2006)

6: Henri Nouwen, *The Return of the Prodigal Son* (London: Darton, Longman & Todd, 1994)

7: Viktor E. Frankl, *Man's Search for Meaning* (London: Random House, 2004)

8: Thomas Keating, *Open Mind, Open Heart* (London: Bloomsbury, 2006)

9: Brother Roger Schutz, quoted in *The Youth Catechism of the Catholic Church* (San Francisco: Ignatius Press, 2011)

10: Saint John Paul II, *Novo Millennio Ineunte* http://w2.vatican.va/content/john-paul-ii/en/apost_letters/2001/documents/hf_jp-ii_apl_20010106_novo-millennio-ineunte.html, accessed 9 April 2015

11: Karl Rahner, *Christians Living Formerly and Today, Theological Investigations VII*, trans. David Bourke (New York: Herder and Herder, 1971)

12: Karl Rahner, Secular Life and the Sacraments: A Copernican Revolution, *The Tablet* (6 and 13 March, 1971)

13: http://www.wcr.ab.ca/WCRThisWeek/Stories/tabid/61/entryid/984/Default.aspx, accessed 3 January 2015

14: Heythrop Institute for Religion, Ethics and Public Life, *On the Way to Life* (London: Catholic Education Service, 2005)

15: St Augustine, *Confessions* (London: Penguin Classics, 2002)

16: Philip Larkin, "Faith Healing" from *Collected Poems* (London: Faber & Faber, 1990)

17: Viktor E. Frankl, *Man's Search for Meaning* (London: Random House, 2004)

18: Thomas Merton, *Love and Living* (New York: Farrar, Straus & Giroux, 1979)

19: St Paul, Second Letter to the Corinthians 4:7-9

20: Thomas Keating, *Open Mind, Open Heart* (London, Bloomsbury, 2006)

21: Oscar Romero, *Through the Year with Oscar Romero: Daily Meditations* (London: Darton, Longman & Todd, 2006)

22: Isaiah 58:6-8

23: Viktor E. Frankl, *Man's Search for Meaning* (London: Random House, 2004)

24: Oscar Romero, *Through the Year with Oscar Romero: Daily Meditations* (London: Darton, Longman & Todd, 2006)

25: Thomas Keating, *Open Mind, Open Heart* (London, Bloomsbury, 2006)

26: C.S. Lewis, *The Weight of Glory* (London: William Collins, 2013)

27: St John's Gospel 1:1-5

28: First Epistle of John 4:4

29: Thomas Keating, *Open Mind, Open Heart* (London, Bloomsbury, 2006)

30: Julian of Norwich, *Revelations of Divine Love* (London: Penguin Classics, 1998)

31: Marilynne Robinson, *Gilead* (London: Virago, 2005)

32: Viktor Frankl, *Man's Search for Meaning* (London: Random House, 2004)

33: St Paul, Second Letter to the Corinthians 5:14-21